MW00399257

The Crisis
of Police Liability Lawsuits

Prevention and Management

Walter P. Signorelli, Esq.

CAROLINA ACADEMIC PRESS
Durham, North Carolina

Copyright © 2006
Walter P. Signorelli, Esq.
All Rights Reserved

Library of Congress Cataloging-in-Publication Data

Signorelli, Walter P.

The crisis of police liability lawsuits : prevention and management / by Walter P. Signorelli, Esq.

p. cm.

Includes index.

ISBN 1-59460-228-X

1. Tort liability of police--United States. I. Title.

KF1307.S545 2006

344.7305'2--dc22

2006012316

Carolina Academic Press
700 Kent Street
Durham, North Carolina 27701
Telephone (919) 489-7486
Fax (919) 493-5668
www.cap-press.com

Printed in the United States of America

Table of Contents

About the Author

Walter Signorelli was a member of the New York City Police Department for thirty-one years. He served in ranks from police officer to inspector, held positions as the commanding officer of precincts in Brooklyn and Manhattan, and as an executive officer in the Detective Bureau, the Organized Crime Control Bureau, and the Narcotics Division. He is a graduate of St. John's University School of Law, cum laude, and of the Columbia University Police Management Institute. Since his retirement from the police department in 1998, he has practiced law and acted as a police practices consultant and expert witness for both plaintiffs and defendants in numerous police-liability lawsuits. Currently, he is an adjunct professor of law and police science at John Jay College of Criminal Justice and at St. John's University, School of Professional Studies.

Introduction

While I was a member of the New York City Police Department from 1967 to 1998, I was well aware of the hazards police officers faced from potential lawsuits, but I did not realize the full extent of police vulnerability until I retired and became a participant in the lawsuit process. During my practice as an attorney and a consultant, I have noted the dramatic increase in the number of lawsuits against police, the expanding types of theories on which to sue, and the exorbitant jury awards given to some undeserving plaintiffs. I have also noticed the patterns of recurring mistakes made by officers—mistakes that have allowed attorneys to prove liability even when the officers had acted in good faith and in accordance with their responsibilities.

Many lawsuits against the police are justified and serve the purpose of obtaining compensation for injured plaintiffs. Many more are unjustified, and proceed through the legal system only because police officers have been ill prepared to defend themselves and their departments. Some of the more egregious cases that have resulted in coerced settlements or unjust verdicts against the police have encouraged further lawsuits. As the number of successful lawsuits increases, the implications for law enforcement are profound. Levels of police morale, public confidence, and the recruitment of qualified candidates are showing severe signs deterioration.

The explosion of federal lawsuits through civil rights actions has magnified the problem, and has increased the potential liability of police supervisors, agencies, and the municipalities that employ them.

A premise of this book is that police officers are unnecessarily losing cases through inadequate awareness and preparation, and they unwittingly provide the ammunition for attorneys to use against them.

I attempt to raise awareness of these critical issues and to instruct law enforcement personnel regarding the risks they take and the common mistakes that increase their vulnerability. The book is also designed to train officers on how to conduct themselves during deposition examinations and trial testimony. Several chapters discuss the differences between criminal law, state tort law, and federal civil rights litigation, and the different roles police officers play in each category. The history and more recent developments of police-liability law are outlined.

Actual case summaries and transcripts of testimony are used as examples. Some of these have been abridged and altered to avoid the unnecessary identification of the participants. These examples illustrate the tactics used by attorneys to undermine the credibility and positions of police witnesses. They also illustrate proper and improper responses that police witnesses have given, and the results of these responses.

Police practices and procedures that tend to expose police agencies to liability are discussed. The exclusionary rule in criminal law, tailored testimony, and the disastrous consequences of even minor falsehoods are highlighted. Finally, strategies and recommendations for changes that will help prevent liability are offered.

The information and materials in this book are presented for general discussion, training, and educational purposes only and are not meant to be a source of legal advice to be applied to a particular case. Law enforcement officers and agencies should consult their attorneys for specific legal advice.

CHAPTER ONE

The Battle

American law enforcement is in the midst of a battle to maintain its integrity, authority, and effectiveness. This battle has been brought about by battalions of attorneys filing barrages of lawsuits on behalf of plaintiffs alleging police abuse or negligence. Although many of these lawsuits are justified, the majority are not; and many of the unjustified lawsuits result in monetary judgments or settlements against the police. The explosion in the number of police-liability lawsuits is contributing to a loss of confidence in the police and is discouraging qualified individuals from choosing law enforcement as a career.[1] These lawsuits are causing law-enforcement policy makers to restrict the use of police authority and to limit the discretionary powers of police officers. Paradoxically, the restrictions and limitations are not reducing lawsuits but are creating new grounds for litigation.

Our civil court system is an essential strength of the nation. When an individual is physically or financially injured by the intentional, reckless, or negligent conduct of another, he or she has a right to bring an action to redress the wrong. Currently, however, our civil courts are subject to abuse and are burdened with too many unwarranted cases. The overwhelming majority of these cases are filed against entities that have the assets or insurance coverage to afford payment of large monetary sums; rarely are such cases filed against someone without sufficient means to pay. Police departments and the governmental agencies that fund them have the "deep pockets" that attorneys look for when filing lawsuits, and since police action inherently involves conflict, restraint, force, and injury, it provides the material from which attorneys can develop lucrative cases. Consequently, police increasingly find themselves as defendants.

Why do some lawyers file unwarranted lawsuits against the police? They do so because they are aware of the strong antipolice bias in parts of the pop-

---

1. "Police Departments Struggle to Find Recruits," *Detroit News*, June 3, 2000; "Struggle to Find the Next Generation," *USA Today*, Nov. 20, 2000; Kevin Flynn, "Flaws Seen in Effort to Fill Police Class," *New York Times*, July 2, 2001.

ulation. They also know that police officers, while handling difficult and unpredictable situations, invariably make substantive or procedural errors that can be used to portray an individual officer or an entire department as incompetent or malevolent. Since police officers are action oriented, focused on their perceived mission, and not self-critical, they are vulnerable to second-guessing by experienced and articulate attorneys who can persuade juries that the police did something wrong.

Although police officers are generally trained to present evidence in criminal courts against criminal defendants, they are ill prepared for civil lawsuits in which they, the police, are the defendants. During the course of their professional activities, the police take action, write reports, and provide testimony. They do all this without the benefit of advice from counsel regarding the legal liabilities that they may incur. In the event of a subsequent suit, the police have already made the mistakes and omissions that provide ammunition for plaintiff attorneys. Then they face the difficulty of switching from being prosecution witnesses in criminal court to being defendants in civil court, and in so doing, they commit additional mistakes that provide additional material for attorneys to use against them.

Every year in the United States, approximately 30,000 lawsuits are filed against police officers, their departments, municipalities, or counties. The amount of money paid for verdicts and settlements is difficult to verify, but it is in the millions of dollars—millions that could have been used for other needed government services or for more resources to fight crime. Some areas of the country are paying out higher amounts and more frequently than others. In such areas a cyclical effect has been created in which the more money that is paid out, the more lawsuits are filed. The floodgates have been opened, and lawyers have poured in, some filing borderline and even frivolous lawsuits, hoping for a quick and easy settlement.

For example, in New York City, in 2005, more than 1100 police-related tort cases were filed against the New York City Police Department, and 11,000 cases were pending from prior years.[2]

To defend them all, the city would require an army of attorneys and supporting staff; instead 94 percent of the cases will be settled. Thus, if a lawyer can marshal sufficient facts to get a case past a motion for dismissal, the case will most likely be settled.

Of the 6 percent of the cases that go to trial, the City wins about half, representing a score of 97 to 3 for the plaintiffs.

---

2. New York City Law Department, "Tort Reform," www.nyc.gov/html/law.com.

The police response to the onslaught of liability lawsuits has been self-restriction and the promulgation of written policies explaining the restrictions. Following lawsuits for deaths caused by choke holds, many police departments banned choke holds; after injuries caused by high-speed chases, high-speed chases were restricted; after injuries to fleeing violent felons, the use of deadly force to apprehend fleeing violent felons was banned. This growing list of self-restrictive policies creates additional opportunities for lawyers to sue.

Self-restriction has been an ineffective response. It does not address the core issue of the conflicts between the police and the public that are inherent in the nature of police work and the ongoing challenges to the ability of the police to perform their required functions and fulfill their responsibilities to public safety. Law enforcement needs to recognize the developing challenges, investigate the causes, and find pragmatic and lawful solutions, just as it has done with challenges in the past.

One such challenge arose when the United States Supreme Court imposed the exclusionary rule and other legal technicalities on law enforcement. In such cases as *Mapp v. Ohio*, 367 U.S. 643 (1961) and *Miranda v. Arizona*, 384 U.S. 436 (1966), the Court attempted to deter the police from violating constitutional rights by setting the rule that evidence obtained in violation of the constitutional would not be admissible in court. Some observers predicted that the exclusionary rule, as applied by the Supreme Court and as interpreted and expanded by lower courts, would result in handcuffing the police. The facts have not borne out the predictions. Although the exclusionary rule has caused the police to adjust their procedures, it has not stopped the police from doing their jobs. Law enforcement has been active and relatively effective. With improved training, forensics, and technology, law enforcement has maintained its capabilities and has overcome the challenge of the exclusionary rule.

However, law enforcement has not adequately or effectively responded to the challenge of police-liability lawsuits. By sheer numbers and financial impact, these lawsuits are becoming a much greater constraint on police performance than the so-called handcuffs of the exclusionary rule. The exclusion of evidence from a criminal proceeding has only an indirect effect on the police in that guilty criminals unjustly avoid punishment because of a dismissal or a plea bargain to a lesser charge. On the other hand, police-liability lawsuits have a direct effect. They can result in monetary damages against individual officers and police agencies whether or not the plaintiffs were guilty of a crime or committed a dangerous act that had precipitated the police action in question. These lawsuits make the police vulnerable even when they act with good intentions and within the scope of their duties;

moreover, these lawsuits are having a serious negative impact on police morale and capabilities.

Ostensibly, the public policy behind these lawsuits is to deter police from repeating injurious behavior, and many lawyers see themselves as protecting the rights of people abused by police misconduct. No doubt, there is some truth in that. However, the primary purpose of most police-liability lawsuits is for lawyers to make money at the expense of vulnerable and ill-prepared police departments. Lawyers who accumulate fortunes suing police departments rationalize that they are bringing about positive change, but most would not be gratified to find that police officers had somehow found a way to perform their duties in the absence of mistakes, conflicts, or the use of force.

In recent years, scores of cases in which the police were accused of mistakes, excessive force, or outright brutality have received national prominence and, rightly or wrongly, are now ingrained into the public mind as clear proof of endemic and widespread police misconduct. Three infamous cases were the 1991 videotaped police beating of Rodney King that led to riots in Los Angeles, the 1997 broom-handle sodomy of Abner Louima in a Brooklyn police station, and the 1999 New York City incident in which four plainclothes police officers fired forty-one shots at an unarmed immigrant, Amadou Diallo, and killed him because he was "acting suspiciously" and they "thought he was armed with a gun."[3] Such cases have allowed lawyers to establish a beachhead from which they can mount offensives against the police. Although these cases certainly make clear the need for close scrutiny of police action and the need to protect the right of citizens to bring lawsuits against police officers and police departments, the negative public perception engendered by these cases supports the growing movement to file unwarranted lawsuits against the police and buoys the theories under which one may sue the police. This negative view of the police finds its way into jury rooms and is a major reason why juries are so often willing to find the police at fault. This circumstance in turn encourages attorneys to file more lawsuits, many of which are frivolous, contemptuous, and misguided.

In New York City alone there are numerous examples of unwarranted lawsuits filed against the police that have proceeded through the courts and resulted in settlements or verdicts in favor of the plaintiffs. In one recent case, the plaintiff, a drug dealer with a long arrest record, had just made a sale of

---

3. Michael Cooper, "Officers in Bronx Fire 41 Shots, and an Unarmed Man is Killed," *New York Times*, February 4, 1999.

crack cocaine to an undercover officer on a Bronx street. When an officer attempted to arrest the drug dealer, he attacked the officer, took the officer's service revolver, and pointed it at him. Before the drug dealer was able to pull the trigger, the officer was able to pull out his backup gun just in time to shoot and kill him. The police department investigation of the shooting found that the officer acted properly and justifiably. A grand jury reviewed the evidence and cleared the officer. Nonetheless, an attorney for the drug dealer's family sued the police for unnecessary force and collected a large settlement.[4]

In another case, the plaintiff, who had been recently paroled for an attempted manslaughter conviction, was wanted for a newly committed murder in which he had shot a man in the heart. While the plaintiff was on the run and hiding from the police and parole authorities, he was tracked to an apartment in a Queens, New York, housing development. A contingent of police, including two sergeants, entered the apartment to search for him. The sergeants spotted his foot sticking out from under a pile of clothes in a closet. When they reached down to pull him out of the closet, he shot both sergeants several times with an automatic weapon. Although one sergeant was lying seriously wounded in front of the closet, he was able to fire numerous shots into the closet to prevent the plaintiff from shooting him or the other sergeant again. The other sergeant was shot in the right hand, and the bullet magazine of his gun was damaged by the bullet. He had to retreat to reload his gun, then returned and fired into the closet so that he could drag the severely wounded sergeant to safety. Subsequent to his apprehension by responding police officers, the plaintiff was convicted of attempted murder and sentenced to twenty-five years in prison. An attorney representing him has since sued the police for excessive force.[5]

One of the most outlandish cases in the history of police-liability lawsuits was filed on behalf of seven plaintiffs who had been arrested after an incident at Orchard Beach, a city park in the Bronx, New York, on September 7, 1992, Labor Day. The plaintiffs had assembled on the boardwalk to protest against the Budweiser Beer Company, which they claimed discriminated against minority beer distributors. They were on the boardwalk for several hours, holding signs, distributing fliers, walking around, and encouraging passers-by to boycott Budweiser beer. However, the plaintiffs did not have a permit to demonstrate and their conduct violated park regulations.

---

4. *Nelson v. City of New York*, NY Supreme Court (Bronx, Ct.Rpt. Bowles, 1992).
5. *Pritchett v. City of New York*, NY Supreme Court (Queens, Ct.Rpt. D'Amato, 1995).

After several hours, the police instructed them to stop distributing fliers and to cease demonstrating. The plaintiffs refused to comply. Some of the plaintiffs argued with the police and chanted slogans loudly. When asked and then directed by the police to disperse, the demonstrators refused. During the ensuing police attempt to make arrests, the demonstrators resisted arrest, and a brawl followed. A number of plaintiffs knocked a uniformed police sergeant to the ground, and in an attempt to gain control, one police officer struck the primary plaintiff, Idelfonso Rivera, Sr., on the head with a flashlight. The seven plaintiffs were arrested. Four were charged with assault and disorderly conduct, and three were charged with disorderly conduct only. The latter three were given summonses and released immediately. The four charged with assault were kept in custody, processed, and released at their arraignment within twenty-four hours.

Three years later, the plaintiffs were acquitted of all charges in Bronx Criminal Court. Their subsequent lawsuit against the police for excessive force, false arrest, malicious prosecution, and violation of civil rights was heard in a Bronx civil court.

At the civil-court trial, some of the alleged damages were as follows. Mr. Rivera, Sr., who had been struck with the flashlight, sustained a head laceration that required eighteen stitches but left no discernable scar. The only other medical treatment he received was removal of the sutures. He was arrested and held in custody until his arraignment. He claimed to have seen a psychologist four or five times after the incident, but no testimony or records to that effect were introduced. Rivera, Sr., claimed he experienced nightmares and was afraid of the police. The plaintiff's expert, Dr. Dudley, who examined him for litigation purposes in the year 2000, eight years after the incident, testified that the plaintiff suffered from posttraumatic stress disorder.

Plaintiff Idelfonso Rivera, Jr., the son of Rivera, Sr., sustained swelling to his face. He was taken to the hospital, where X-rays revealed no fractures. He did not receive any further medical treatment. He was released at his arraignment. Regarding his psychological condition, he made the same claim as his father and presented the same evidence, or lack of evidence. Dr. Dudley testified that Rivera, Jr., also suffered from posttraumatic stress disorder.

Plaintiff Lorenzo Rivera suffered no injuries and received no medical or psychological treatment. He was released at his arraignment. Dr. Dudley testified that Lorenzo Rivera, too, suffered from posttraumatic stress disorder.

Plaintiff Raphael Marrero claimed he was struck in the head. He was taken to the hospital, but no medical records were offered into evidence. He was released at his arraignment. Coincidentally, Dr. Dudley testified that Marrero suffered from posttraumatic stress disorder.

Of the three plaintiffs who were issued summonses and released—Kelvin Gonzalez, Martin Torres, and David Andino—none received any medical or psychological treatment, although Dr. Dudley testified that all three suffered posttraumatic stress disorder.

On the basis of the above information, a Bronx jury, in 2004, rendered a verdict in favor of the plaintiffs. In total, they awarded the plaintiffs $81 million. Rivera, Sr., who had received eighteen stitches, was awarded $30 million. Rivera, Jr., who had had facial swelling, was awarded $3 million. Lorenzo Rivera, who had received no medical or psychological treatment, was awarded $15 million. Marrero was awarded $15 million. Gonzalez, who had received no medical or psychological treatment but had been given a summons, received an award of $10 million. Torres was awarded $5 million. Andino received an award of only $3 million.[6]

When people are given the power to punish without restraint, they sometimes exercise that power, as this jury did.

In response to post verdict motions or appeals, these jury awards may be reduced as excessive by the trial judge or an appellant court, but the damage to the police, the system, and the individual officers involved has already been done.

The above are just a few examples of the thousands of unwarranted lawsuits filed against the police and the exorbitant amounts of money awarded. The injustice of such lawsuits and awards to undeserving plaintiffs and attorneys at the expense of police officers and law-enforcement agencies undermines police morale and diminishes respect for the law and the jury system. Moreover, these lawsuits disseminate false information to the public that the police are incompetent, corrupt, brutal, or racist. Certainly, a few officers out of many need to be dismissed, but all police officers should not be painted as malevolent. Many plaintiff attorneys propagate the idea that the police always lie, always cover up. Whether by direct attack, or by innuendo, such attorneys destroy the credibility of entire police departments and convince juries to "pay back" the police—to punish them by awarding huge amounts of money to supposedly aggrieved plaintiffs. Law enforcement has an obligation to mount a defense against this attack. It has to fight the battle against crime, injustice, and cynicism not only in the criminal courts but also in the civil courts.

---

6. *Idelfonso Rivera et al. v. City of New York*, NY Supreme Court (Bronx, Ct.Rpt. Barrett, 1993).

Law enforcement must recognize the mind-set, methods, and tactics of the attorneys who file unwarranted lawsuits and must train its officers to understand and counteract them.

Trial lawyers are in an odd profession. They are required to argue zealously on behalf of their clients, though in many situations they know the client's position is not entirely correct or truthful. To win cases, they often use their skills to mislead, to hide some facts, or to exaggerate others. This is called *fact management*, and lawyers do not see this as dishonest but as their duty. When the facts of a case are clearly on their side, lawyers can be honest. If, however, as in most cases that go to trial, there is controversy over the facts, they will arrange or emphasize the facts in a manner that will prove their version of the case or disprove their opponent's version. The end result is a reinvention of the facts into a story as false as true.

When they have a weak case, some lawyers will invent facts. Because they cannot readily invent physical facts, they invent attitudinal facts. They raise perception and credibility issues.

This is nothing new to the legal profession. Cicero, the great Roman advocate, wrote about the judicial process: "The judges' business, in every trial, is to discover the truth. As for counsel, however, he may on occasion have to base his advocacy on points which *look like* the truth, even if they do not correspond with it exactly."[7]

In police-liability cases, the same well-known tactics used by criminal-defense attorneys to raise a "reasonable doubt" are modified for use in civil lawsuits: Attack the victim, allege a police frame-up, or assert that the crime-scene technicians bungled the handling of the physical evidence. Facts are managed or invented to show police incompetence, prejudice, or cover-up. Lawyers will tap into the negative information the public has received about police from news stories, television, Hollywood, and well-known cases of egregious police abuse. They wager that jurors will connect their case with the body of negative material about police that permeates the public mind.

It is beyond the scope of this book to describe how it has come about that so many lawyers are willing to engage in such questionable practices and are so willing to view the law-enforcement community and the judicial system from such a negative perspective. But some of the brightest lights of the legal profession have provided insight into the question.

---

7. Marcus Tullius Cicero, *On Duties, II*, trans. Michael Grant in *Cicero on the Good Life*, (New York: Penguin Classics, 1971) 147.

Perhaps the most famous lawyer in American history was Clarence Darrow, The Great Defender. He defended more than 100 murderers, including Leopold and Loeb in 1926. Darrow's claim to fame was that although some of his clients were guilty, none of them were executed. He became a model for trial attorneys, and in fact, his moral philosophy, or lack thereof, represents the cynical views of many criminal-defense attorneys and police-liability lawyers.

Darrow made many speeches and was very quotable. When asked about justice, he replied, "Is there anybody who knows what justice is? No one of earth can measure out justice. Can you look at any man and say what he deserves—whether he deserves hanging by the neck until dead or life in prison or thirty days or a medal?"[8]

Darrow rejected the concept of law as anything but the exercise of power: "I don't want to dispute with him about the right of the state to kill people. Of course, they have got a right to kill them.... That is, they have got the power. And you have got a right to do what you get away with. The words power and right, so far as this is concerned, mean exactly the same thing."[9]

Darrow viewed humans not as moral entities possessing true freedom of choice but as the subjects of determinism. He claimed: "All people are products of two things, and two things only—their heredity and their environment. And they act in exact accord with the heredity which they took from all the past, and for which they are in no wise responsible, and the environment.... We all act from the same way."[10]

If anything, Darrow was consistent. In 1936, at eighty years of age and near the end of his life, he gave an interview to the *New York Times* in which he stated, "There is no such thing as justice—in or out of court."[11] Darrow's cynicism, his belief in determinism and moral relativism, his disbelief in justice, have all been inculcated into our culture, into our justice system, and particularly into the minds of many attorneys.

Police officers should understand not only the tactics of certain lawyers but also the foundations of their mentality. Darrow's dismissal of justice as an achievable goal was a precursor to today's win-by-any-means-possible

---

8. Arthur Weinberg, *Attorney for the Damned*, (New York: Simon and Schuster, 1957), 95.

9. Ibid. at 93.

10. Ibid. at 98.

11. "Law is Horrible, Says Darrow," *New York Times*, April 19, 1936.

mentality. When lawyers can deny responsibility for achieving justice, their only rule is to obtain a win for their side.

In 1967, Supreme Court Justice Byron White, in a dissenting opinion in *U.S. v Wade*, 388 U.S. 218, compared the roles of law enforcement versus defense attorneys:

> Law enforcement have the obligation to convict the guilty and to make sure they do not convict the innocent. They must be dedicated to making the criminal trial a procedure for the ascertainment of the true facts surrounding the commission of the crime. To this extent, our so-called adversary system is not adversarial at all; nor should it be. But defense counsel has no comparable obligation to ascertain or present the truth. Our system assigns him a different mission. He must be and is interested in preventing the conviction of the innocent, but, absent a voluntary plea of guilty, we also insist that he defend his client whether he is innocent or guilty. The State has the obligation to present the evidence. Defense counsel need present nothing, even if he knows what the truth is. He need not furnish any witnesses to the police, or reveal any confidences of his client, or furnish any other information to help the prosecution's case. If he can confuse a witness, even a truthful one, or make him appear at a disadvantage, unsure or indecisive, that will be his normal course. Our interest in not convicting the innocent permits counsel to put the State to its proof, to put the State's case in the worst possible light, regardless of what he thinks or knows to be the truth. Undoubtedly there are some limits which defense counsel must observe but more often than not, defense counsel will cross-examine a prosecution witness, and impeach him if he can, even if he thinks the witness is telling the truth, just as he will attempt to destroy a witness he thinks is lying. In this respect, as part of our modified adversary system and as part of the duty imposed on the most honorable defense counsel, we countenance or require conduct which in many instances has little, if any, relation to the search for truth.

Police-liability attorneys, although they have the burden of proof and must bring forth evidence, employ and rely on the same approaches and methods as criminal-defense attorneys. The tactics allowed for protecting criminal defendants and ensuring that the innocent are not convicted are transported into the civil realm and used to assail defendant police officers. The police must recognize how extremely adversarial the process can become and the extent to which they are prime targets for such lawyers.

CHAPTER TWO

Differences Between Criminal and Civil Actions

Law-enforcement officers, whether defendants or witnesses in police-liability lawsuits, need to understand the differences between the two spheres of the judicial system: criminal law and civil law. No doubt they understand that the purpose of criminal law is to deter prohibited conduct by the threat or the imposition of prison sentences. The purpose of civil law is to settle disputes and to provide a remedy for personal and financial injuries, usually by awarding a monetary award. High standards of proof must be met to obtain a criminal conviction, and the criminal defendant can invoke substantial privileges and protections. To obtain a civil-liability verdict, the standards are much lower, and the civil defendant has fewer privileges and protections. A criminal conviction can be based only on a clearly defined statute that was in effect prior to the conduct; a civil judgment can be based on broad, general concepts that can be applied after the fact and can be applied in different ways at different times.

Standards of Proof

A criminal conviction must be based on proof beyond a reasonable doubt, an extremely high standard designed to reduce the probability of sending an innocent person to prison. Proof beyond a reasonable doubt must be of such a convincing character that a juror would be willing to rely and act on it unhesitatingly. If a juror thinks there is a real possibility that the defendant is not guilty, the juror must give the defendant the benefit of the doubt with a finding of not guilty.

In a civil case, a verdict can be based on a preponderance of the evidence, which has been defined as an amount of evidence that establishes the contested fact as more probably true than not true. It has been said that 51 percent of the evidence in favor of a plaintiff is a preponderance of the evidence that will support a verdict of liability. This more lenient standard is used because civil law evolved as the means to settle disputes over contractual matters or claims for compensation for financial or personal injury. Unfortunately for police-officer defendants, this lower standard of proof makes winning a case against them relatively easy.

The factual issues in civil police-liability cases are more often comparable to the factual issues in criminal cases, such as justification, self-defense, or unlawful imprisonment than they are to civil contractual law or negligence law. Yet police officers have to defend themselves without the protection of the beyond-a-reasonable-doubt standard.

Self-incrimination

In criminal cases, defendants cannot be compelled to testify against themselves. They have a right to remain silent at their trial and at all times before their trial. Even when defendants fail to offer an explanation of their actions or movements under circumstances in which an innocent person would surely do so, such failure cannot be used to infer their guilt.[1]

On the other hand, in a civil case, a defendant does not have the right to remain silent. His refusal to answer or testify may result in a default judgment, an adverse inference against him, or other sanctions.[2]

Summons and Complaint

In criminal court a defendant does not have to act affirmatively (other than making court appearances) and does not have to mount a defense or answer questions or submit written documents. He or she can remain silent and wait for the prosecution to prove the case. A civil-lawsuit defendant must act affirmatively and immediately. When served with a civil-court summons, the defendant must answer the allegations in writing within a limited time. If he fails to do so, a default judgment may be entered, and the defendant will be liable for the amount of money claimed.

When police officers are served with a summons for actions within the scope of their employment, they must notify their agency and obtain legal representation from the agency. In cases wherein the agency believes the officer acted outside the scope of his or her employment, the agency may de-

---

1. *Malloy v. Hogan*, 378 U.S. 1 (1964).
2. *Baxter v. Palmigiano*, 425 U.S. 308 (1976).

cline to represent the officer and decline to indemnify the officer against any judgment. In such an event, the officer must obtain his own counsel, and the officer should realize that he or she could be held liable for any monetary judgment.

Pretrial Discovery

In a criminal case, pretrial discovery is limited. The district attorney must provide any known exculpatory evidence to the defense and copies of prior statements made by witnesses whom he intends to call to testify. The defense, on the other hand, does not have to provide incriminatory evidence to the prosecution but has to notify the prosecution only of the basis for raising an alibi or an insanity defense.

In a civil case, pretrial discovery is designed so that each party will know everything about the case before trial. Parties are subject to the rules of full and open discovery and can be required to submit to oral depositions and written interrogatories. A police-officer defendant can expect to be extensively questioned about his actions, background, training, and motives. The officer can expect that the plaintiff's attorney will do everything possible to get him to implicate himself and provide the basis for his own liability.

Federal Courts

Law-enforcement officers may be sued in federal courts rather than in state courts when the conduct they are charged with involves violations of the United States Constitutional or federal statutes. When federal civil rights claims are filed in federal courts, state claims, such as assault and battery, excessive use of force, false arrest, false imprisonment, unlawful search and seizure, or malicious prosecution, can also be included in the complaint and will be adjudicated by the federal court along with the civil rights claims. One advantage for a plaintiff filing in federal court is that the federal discovery rules allow for even broader discovery inquiry than state courts.

Penalties and Damages

Civil-liability verdicts generally involve compensatory damages to the victim for the injury caused by the defendant. If a police officer who was found liable for the injury had acted within the scope of his employment, most likely he would be indemnified by the agency, and the agency would pay the judgment.

However, if a jury imposed punitive damages on an officer, his agency may not legally indemnify him. Punitive damages are designed to penalize, and indemnification would nullify the penalty. Although a police officer who is found liable would not be subject to a prison sentence, he may be required to pay an onerous financial judgment that can be even more devastating than a prison sentence. The law holds that punitive damages should be imposed for intentionally abusive or particularly egregious conduct only, but regardless of the law, juries regularly award punitive damages when the police conduct was merely negligent. Individual officers should understand that if they are found personally liable and a judgment of punitive damages is imposed on them, they may not be indemnified by their agency and will have to pay the judgment themselves.

In some instances, juries award compensatory damages only, but the enormous amounts of the awards are inherently punitive, even though they may not be labeled as such. In these instances, the municipality indemnifying the officer is punished.

Liability for Conduct of Others

In criminal law, a person does not have an obligation to intercede to prevent a crime or to render aid to an injured person. When another person commits a crime, an individual can be criminally liable for that crime only by soliciting, requesting, commanding, or intentionally aiding the other person to engage in the conduct.

In civil law, police officers can be held liable for the conduct of other officers merely by their presence during the occurrence of the offending conduct. An officer can be liable for failure to intercede to prevent another police officer from assaulting a person or violating a person's constitutional rights. When officers act together in a group, an officer who is not culpable can be held liable for the conduct of another officer who fires his weapon in violation of a person's constitutional rights.[3]

---

3. *Gutierrez-Rodriguez v .Cartagena,*, 882 F.2d 553 (1st Cir. 1989).

Depositions

Depositions are a critical part of the investigative and discovery process in civil cases. Contrary to common belief, the deposition, not the trial, is usually the most significant event in a lawsuit. The main purposes of the deposition are as follows:

    a.   To obtain information.
    b.   To preserve testimony.
    c.   To compel a party or nonparty witness to commit to a position.
    d.   To establish a basis for impeachment in cross-examination at trial.
    e.   To authenticate documents.
    f.   To obtain evidence for use at trial.

The discovery rules pertaining to depositions have evolved to permit broad, wide-ranging inquiry and what some would call "fishing expeditions" for information. Witnesses must answer questions unless

    a.   they are protected by constitutional privilege; or
    b.   they are protected by recognized common law or statutory privilege, such as husband-wife, attorney-client, or doctor-patient privilege; or
    c.   the question is "palpably" or "grossly" irrelevant.

In a criminal case, a defendant cannot be compelled to testify against himself, and a judge is present at pretrial appearances and hearings to protect a defendant's rights. In a civil case, defendants can be compelled to testify at the trial or before the trial at depositions. A judge is not present at a civil deposition, except in rare circumstances. Generally, the defendant, his lawyer, the opposing lawyer, and a notary/stenographer are present. The plaintiff has a right to attend. The defendant must testify under oath, and the questions and answers will be recorded, sometimes videotaped. A defendant who does not testify may jeopardize his position. The judge may order a default judgment, strike parts or all of the defendant's answer to the complaint, preclude testimony, or order other sanctions. If a police-officer defendant raises his Fifth Amendment right against self-incrimination and refuses to testify during a deposition, the trial court may subsequently prevent him from testifying on his own behalf during the trial.[4] *Gutierrez-Rodriguez v. Cartagena, supra.*

---

4. *Gutierrez-Rodriguez*, 882 F.2d 553.

Nonparty witnesses who ignore a subpoena or refuse an order to testify can be held in contempt of court.

The deposition is a pivotal event wherein the interrogating attorney unearths the facts and knowledge he needs to prove the case or, at least, the material needed to contradict a witness at trial. The attorney will use whatever strategy is necessary to gather information, to pin down a witness to a specific position, and, if possible, to obtain incriminating admissions.

The deposition of a police-officer defendant is an important event for plaintiff attorneys who have invested a lot of time and energy preparing for this stage. Therefore, an officer who is going to be deposed should be aware that the plaintiff attorney has obtained all available records and prior statements pertaining to the case. The attorney will have scrutinized all of the officer's reports, looking for mistakes, conflicts, inconsistencies, and omissions.

In police-liability cases, most often the pivotal issue is whether or not the jury will believe the police version of the event. Therefore, attorneys who specialize in police-liability cases are always prepared and willing to destroy a police officer's credibility. The attorney will have documents that are effective tools for cross-examination, but it is difficult to convince a jury with documents only. Documents can be confusing or unconvincing. The attorney needs to put flesh on the bones of his evidence. He needs a live body, and in order to win, he often has to make the live body—the officer—look like a fool or a malicious, brutal, or racist cop.

The attorney may attempt to accomplish this portrayal during the deposition or may just set the groundwork and finish the job during the trial. Police officers must always remember that no matter how solicitous or friendly the plaintiff's attorney appears, he or she is an adversary who may employ many methods to unnerve, unravel, confuse, and destroy a witness.

In 1902 Francis Wellman wrote a classic text for lawyers, *The Art of Cross-Examination* in which he described his tactics for handling an adversarial witness.

> "As a general rule it is but a waste of time to put questions which will enable him to repeat his original testimony in the sequence in which he first gave it. You can accomplish nothing with him unless you abandon the train of ideas he followed in giving his main story. Select the weakest points in his testimony and the attendant circumstances he would be least likely to prepare for. Do not ask your questions in logical order, lest he invent conveniently as he goes along; but

dodge him about in his story and pin him down to precise answers on all the accidental circumstances indirectly associated with his main narrative. As he begins to invent his answers, put your questions more rapidly, asking many unimportant ones to one important one, and all in the same voice. If he is not telling the truth, and answering from memory and associated ideas rather than from imagination, he will never be able to invent his answers as quickly as you can frame your questions, and at the same time correctly estimate the bearing his present answer may have upon those that have preceded it. If you have the requisite skill to pursue this method of questioning, you will be sure to land him in a maze of self-contradictions from which he will never be able to extricate himself."[5]

Wellman, in accord with the purposes of cross-examination, employed his skills to uncover witnesses who were "not telling the truth." However, these same skills can be used to confuse and generate contradictions from witnesses who are not lying, who are trying to tell the truth as they know it, but who may have less than perfect memories or had a faulty perception or interpretation of the event. In civil cases, police officers, ironically, are particularly vulnerable to cross-examination tactics. Officers involved in a police incident are expected to have an accurate perception, memory, and interpretation of what occurred, over and above what would be expected from an ordinary citizen. This expectation is not always justified because the officer may be called to testify many years after the fact, and the incident might have been just one of hundreds of similar incidents in which the officer was involved. A private citizen involved in a police incident, especially one who has filed suit, is much more likely to remember the details and much more likely to develop a consistent narrative of the event from his or her point of view. An officer might have handled the same kind of event and filed the same kind of report many times. After the event, the officer might have forgotten about it until he or she was notified to appear at a scheduled deposition.

At a deposition, the examination of a witness can be even more onerous and devastating than at a trial. Under the broad rules of discovery and depo-

---

5. Francis Wellman, *The Art of Cross-Examination* (New York: MacMillan, 1936), 135-36.

Reprinted with the permission of Scribner, an imprint of Simon & Schuster Adult Publishing Group, from *The Art of Cross-Examination* by Francis Wellman. Copyright 1936 by the MacMillan Company; copyright renewed 1964 by Ethel Wellman.

sition, an attorney has great leeway to ask questions of the witness, as long as the questions do not invade a privilege or are not palpably or grossly irrelevant. Such rules create a much wider latitude than the attorney has at trial, where stricter rules of evidence are applied. The attorney can use aggressive tactics and can take risks that he would not ordinarily take in front of a judge and jury. At trial, questions must be relevant and material, and judges can limit them further for practical reasons or because they are badgering, prejudicial, or redundant. However, during a deposition a judge is not present to limit the scope of questioning or restrain an overzealous attorney.

Usually, an officer will be represented by an attorney from the governmental agency that employs him. This attorney can attempt to limit inappropriate questioning and can call the judge for a ruling when he believes the plaintiff's attorney is violating the rules of discovery. But the officer's attorney cannot completely protect him. In all but rare instances, the officer must answer the questions. Therefore, before the deposition, the officer must be fully prepared: first, by reviewing the facts of the case, including his prior reports and statements; second, by anticipating the tactics the opposing attorney may employ; and, third, by considering how best to respond to those tactics.

In addition, police officers should have a satisfactory and working knowledge of civil law and procedure. It is difficult enough to face the deposition process; it is even more difficult to do so without adequate background information. Most people lose confidence when they do not have the knowledge or experience to deal with an unfamiliar subject, and police officers are no different. Although they receive training in criminal law, they also need an understanding of pertinent legal history and how the current focus on police liability has developed.

CHAPTER THREE

The Expansion of Liability and the Dissolution of Defenses

Civil Rights Claims and Municipal Liability

Concurrent with the expansion of protections for criminal defendants brought about by such cases as *Mapp v. Ohio* in 1961 and *Miranda v. Arizona* in 1966, federal courts expanded the methods and theories for bringing civil lawsuits against municipal entities, public officials, and police officers.

In 1961 in *Monroe v. Pape*, 365 U.S. 167, the Supreme Court held that state and local police officers could be personally liable for violations of federal civil-rights law, Title 42, United States Code, Section 1983. This statute had been passed by Congress in 1871 during Reconstruction in order to implement the Thirteen, Fourteenth, and Fifteenth Amendments to the Constitution. Section 1983 states:

> Every person who, under color of any statute, ordinance, regulation, custom, or usage, of any state or territory, subjects or causes to be subjected any citizen of the United States or person within the jurisdiction thereof to the deprivation of any rights, privileges, or immunities secured by the Constitution and the laws, shall be liable to the party injured in an action at law, suit in equity, or other proper proceeding for redress.

Monroe v. Pape ignited a revolution against officials acting under color of state law. Non-prisoner civil-rights actions increased from 150 in 1961 to 42,354 in 1998.[1] Almost any police-related action police officers take, even while they are off-duty, falls within the definition of acting under color of state law. Consequently, any police-related action subjects officers to the scrutiny of Section 1983.

---

1. Theodore Eisenberg, *Civil Rights Litigation*, 5th Ed. (New York: Matthew Bender, 2004), 170.

Monroe was clearly a case that called for a severe remedy. During the investigation of a murder, thirteen police officers kicked in the door and entered the home of the plaintiff, where he, his wife, and children were sleeping. The officers did not have an arrest or search warrant. They ransacked the house and physically abused the plaintiff, his wife, and children. The plaintiff was taken to the police station, where he was interrogated for ten hours. He was subsequently released without charges.

In the civil suit that followed, the officers were found liable for their actions, and a judgment of $13,000 was awarded against them. In hindsight, this was mild compared with today's judgments, but the judgment was against the officers personally. At that time, the Court ruled that municipalities were not "persons" under Section 1983 and could not be liable for the judgment. As a consequence, the ruling provided little motivation to file police-liability lawsuits since individual police officers generally did not have the assets to pay large monetary awards.

In 1971, the Supreme Court, in *Bivens v. Six Unknown Named Agents*, 402 U.S. 388, ruled that federal law-enforcement agents, although not covered by the Section 1983 prohibitions pertaining to persons acting under state law, could be held liable for similar violations of federal constitutional rights. Suits against federal agents could be premised on the Fourth Amendment itself, even without an implementing statute. However, a *Bivens* action can only be brought against the agent individually, not against the United States government or a governmental agency. Since federal agents were unlikely to have any more assets than state or local police officers, lawyers were reluctant to bring expensive and time-consuming suits with only a minimal chance of winning a verdict.

In 1976, to compensate attorneys who filed civil-rights cases against state actors, Congress passed the Attorney's Fees Act, which allowed attorneys who won their suits to collect their reasonable fees and costs without regard to the amount of the award. As a result, when an attorney settled a case even for a moderate amount, he or she could demand a substantial payment from the defendant in addition to the award. This, no doubt, encouraged attorneys to file even the "smallest" cases against those acting under color of state law. Moreover, this did not affect the lawyers' usual one-third contingency fee arrangements with their clients.

Then, in 1978, in *Monell v. Department of Social Services*, 436 U.S. 658, the Supreme Court in part reversed *Monroe* and held that municipalities were "persons" and could be held liable for violations of Section 1983. This decision and others that followed provided the "deep pockets" for lawyers to target. All a lawyer had to do was convince a jury that a police officer, acting under color of state law, violated a person's constitutional rights and that the municipality contributed to the violation by conduct that indicated "deliberate indifference" or "governmental custom." The municipality could be held liable even though the alleged conduct "had not received formal approval through the body's official decision-making channels."

Further, in 1980, in *Owen v. City of Independence*, 445 U.S. 622, the Supreme Court ruled that municipalities could not raise a qualified-immunity defense even when their employees could. The Court reasoned that when a constitutional violation occurred and the individual officials responsible enjoyed qualified immunity, the accountability should shift to the liable municipality so that damages could be paid. In a practical sense, this ruling greatly reduced the protections of qualified immunity.

Monell and *Owen* created a dilemma for police departments and municipalities. When they were included as defendants in civil-rights actions because of a violation by a police officer, they could attempt to extricate themselves from the case by proving that the officer violated department regulations or acted outside the scope of employment and that the municipalities' policies or customs did not contribute to the officer's actions. They knew, however, that if they followed such a path, their police officers would quickly realize that they were being abandoned. Under such circumstances, many police officers would refrain from doing any real police work, and municipalities would be unable to provide for public safety and protection. Consequently, states and municipalities passed laws such as New York State General Municipal Law, Section 50-k, which states in part:

> The city shall save harmless and indemnify any member from financial loss resulting from a proceeding brought in a court of the United States for damages arising out of a negligent act or failure to act or tort which occurred when the member was discharging his duties within the scope of his employment.

The plaintiffs' bar was understandably ecstatic with the passage of such indemnification statutes. A new field of law was born. Municipalities and taxpayers would now become the anonymous providers from whom jurors would have no compunction about extracting large sums of money.

In 1990, federal legislation provided that federal district courts exercising original jurisdiction to hear a Section 1983 claim had the supplemental jurisdiction to adjudicate related state-tort claims that arose out of the same operative facts of the case.[2] This encouraged attorneys to include in their federal actions, using *Monell* municipal liability, such tort claims as negligent hiring, supervision, training, retention, direction, discipline, or investigation.

Section 1983 civil-rights claims can be filed in state courts in conjunction with tort claims, such as negligent police conduct. Many states have liberalized the ability to sue police in their courts, and, as a consequence, many attorneys combine federal and state claims in state courts.

The above developments have created a favorable environment for lawsuits against municipalities. As a result, lawsuits and judgments for plaintiffs have increased dramatically. Between 1978 and 2005, the rate of profit growth for personal injury lawyers who sue municipalities has outpaced any segment of either the stock market or real-estate market. Payments by New York City alone for personal injury cases have risen from $21.4 million in 1978 to $570 million in 2004.

As the money increased, the theories on which lawsuits could be brought against police officers and police departments multiplied. Police-liability attorneys have taken legitimate theories passed upon by courts and pushed them to new limits. Their goal is to get their case before a sympathetic jury on whatever theory they can.

Federal Nullification of State Law

The landmark decision of *Tennessee v. Garner*, 471 U.S. 1, decided by the Supreme Court in 1985, was an important case that mandated a reasonable and necessary change in police policy. Unfortunately, *Garner* was misused by plaintiff attorneys and lower courts to further undermine the ability of police to defend themselves against liability claims.

At the time of *Garner*, several states, including Tennessee, still had laws on their books authorizing police officers to shoot fleeing felons. In the *Garner* case, two officers had responded to a prowler call. At the scene, a witness told them she had heard glass breaking in the house next door. One of the officers saw a suspect running into the backyard of the house and chased the suspect, Garner, an unarmed fifteen-year-old male. When Garner began to climb a six-foot chain-link fence to escape, the officer shot him in the back of the head, killing him.

---

2. 28 USCA, Section 1367(a).

Although Tennessee law authorized the police to use deadly force to arrest fleeing felons, Garner's family brought suit in federal court alleging the officer violated Garner's constitutional rights. The Supreme Court ruled that the shooting of Garner was an unreasonable seizure in violation of the Fourth Amendment of the Constitution. It was not constitutionally permissible to allow police to shoot and kill unarmed suspects fleeing the scene of minor property crimes.

Nevertheless, in *Garner* the Court was careful not to go beyond the facts of the case, and in its ruling it emphasized that it was not prohibiting police from using deadly force to apprehended violent or armed felons. The Court said, "If the suspect threatens the officer with a weapon or there is probable cause to believe that he has committed a crime involving the infliction or threatened infliction of serious physical harm, deadly force may be used if necessary to prevent escape."[3]

Most other states had modified their use of deadly-force statutes before *Garner*. In New York, for example, a police officer could not use deadly force to make arrests for property crimes or minor assaults but could use deadly physical force to arrest or prevent escape for a felony or attempted felony involving the use or attempted use or threatened imminent use of physical force against a person.[4] The New York statute complied with *Garner* before the case was decided.

New York law granted the authority to use deadly force, but it also provided restrictions. Under the statute, that a police officer is justified in using deadly force to arrest a violent or armed felon does not constitute justification for reckless conduct by such police officer amounting to an offense against innocent persons whom he is not seeking to arrest or retain in custody.[5]

So, an officer should not shoot at a fleeing violent felon if innocent persons would thereby be endangered. However, according to the penal law promulgated by the New York State legislature, if innocent persons are not endangered, an officer may shoot at a fleeing violent felon if it is necessary to prevent his escape. This has been the traditional, common understanding of police duty. Officers are hired to capture violent felons and would be remiss in their duty to permit felons to escape from the crime scene. However, the law has been undermined and negated. Courts, at the urging of personal-in-

---

3. *Garner v. Tennessee*, 471 U.S. 1, 11 (1985).
4. *New York Penal Law*, Section 35.30(1).
5. *New York Penal Law*, Section 35.30(2).

jury lawyers, have usurped the legislature's mandates. Police officers can no longer shoot at violent or armed fleeing felons without risking their careers and personal assets. Although the law may protect them from criminal charges, they are subject to civil-liability awards that can be more draconian than a criminal conviction.

The Supreme Court, in *Graham v. Conner*, 490 U.S. 386, (1989), held that excessive-force claims arising out of investigations or arrests or other seizures raise Fourth Amendment issues and should be judged by a standard of objective reasonableness. The Fourth Amendment would be used to scrutinize not only the probable cause for an arrest or a search but also the manner in which the arrest or search was conducted. The Court noted that there is no precise definition of *objective reasonableness*, but its application required "careful attention to the facts and circumstances of each particular case, including the severity of the crime at issue, whether the suspect poses an immediate threat to the safety of the officers or others, and whether he is actively resisting arrest or attempting to evade arrest by flight."

Police officers have had to learn the hard way that the standards by which they are judged are not their familiar criminal-law statutes but the evolving and ever-changing standards of a hybrid constitutional/personal injury law. They have also learned that the objectively reasonable standard is much easier to apply and articulate in hindsight than during the initial street encounter that led to the use of force.

New York police officers have also learned that they can be held liable for the exact duties they were hired, trained, and directed to perform. *McCummings v. New York City Transit Authority*, 177 A.D. 2d 24, 580 N.Y.S. 2d 931 (1992), and 81 N.Y.2d 923 (1993), was a case of particular note. *McCummings* arose from an incident that occurred in June 1984 when Bernard McCummings, along with two other muggers, attacked Jerome Sandusky, a seventy-two-year-old-man, on a New York City subway platform. As one member of the trio kept watch, the other two punched the elderly gentleman, knocking him to the ground. One mugger held Mr. Sandusky down in a choke hold while McCummings rummaged through his pockets.

This was the kind of mugging that epitomized the crime problem in New York at the time. Crime in 1984 was near an all-time high, and the Transit Authority Police Department had deployed undercover officers to work in anticrime units for the express purpose of preventing such violent crimes or arresting the perpetrators before they escaped the scene of the crime. Police Officer Manuel Rodriguez, who had been assigned to this anticrime duty, heard Sandusky's cry for help and rushed to the crime scene. McCummings, when alerted by a lookout, attempted to escape by running to a staircase, which led to a corridor and into the labyrinthine subway system. Officer Rodriguez chased McCummings and called for him to stop. He then made a split-second discretionary decision that it was necessary to shoot McCummings to prevent his escape. He fired and struck McCummings in the back, severing his spinal cord and rendering him paralyzed from the chest down.

In criminal court, McCummings pled guilty to the robbery. Nevertheless, he sued the officer and the Transit Authority, claiming that Officer Rodriguez violated the Fourth Amendment prohibition against unreasonable seizures and unjustifiably committed the tort of assault and battery. The Transit Authority moved to have the case dismissed on the grounds that the officer was performing his lawful duty and was authorized to use deadly force under the circumstances. The Court denied the motion and allowed the trial to proceed. The jury awarded McCummings $4.3 million.

Undoubtedly, sympathy and emotionalism regarding McCummings' paralysis colored the jury's verdict, and the jury was thus receptive to the arguments of the plaintiff's attorney, who was able to point out the usual discrepancies and inconsistencies in the witnesses' statements and testimony, and from the testimony to imply that the police engaged in misconduct or a cover-up.

Putting jury sympathy aside, from a public-policy standpoint, the important issue is whether the case should have gone to the jury at all. The Transit Authority appealed, but the Appellate Court let the verdict stand. By doing so, they de facto rescinded the law of arrest, which justified the use of deadly force by a police officer to arrest a person for "a felony or an attempt to commit a felony involving the use or attempted use of threatened imminent use of physical force against a person."

The trial judge in *McCummings* erroneously instructed the jury: "Generally under the law it is held by the United States Supreme Court the use of deadly physical force by a police officer is unreasonable and unjustified if it is merely intended to prevent a felon from fleeing from a crime and who poses no *immediate* <emphasis added> threat of serious physical injury or harm to an officer or others."[6]

Neither the New York Penal Law nor the Supreme Court in *Tennessee v. Garner* or *Graham v. Conner* imposed a limitation to *immediate* threat. *Garner* allowed the use of deadly force regarding a flight from "a crime involving

---

6. *McCummings v. New York City Transit Authority*, 177 A.D. 2d 24, 56 (1992).

the infliction or threatened infliction of serious physical harm." *Graham* directed consideration of "the severity of the crime at issue … or attempting to evade arrest by flight." The seriousness and violence of the crime matter. If a person pushes someone in front of a subway train, commits a violent rape, slashes someone's face with a razor, or shoots someone in the head, then drops any weapon he may have had and flees, the police need to shoot that person rather than let him escape.

The mugging and robbery of Mr. Sandusky surely fit within the terms of the statute and the rulings in *Garner* and *Graham*. As a result of this case and others, however, police departments have restricted their officers from using deadly force to apprehended fleeing violent felons and have promulgated written rules disallowing use of deadly force.

It may be argued on grounds analogous to the common-law assumption of risk doctrine that cases like *McCummings* should not be allowed to go before a jury. Assumption of risk means that a plaintiff may not recover compensation for an injury to which he assents or for an injury received when he voluntarily exposed himself to a known and appreciated danger.[7]

McCummings knew that to commit a violent robbery on a New York City subway platform and to resist arrest by running from an armed police officer exposed him to a foreseeable danger. In committing the robbery and resisting the arrest, he assumed the risk of apprehension by use of deadly physical force.

To allow plaintiffs such as McCummings to recover awards works at cross-purposes to the criminal law. Most states, including New York, have felony-murder and felony-assault statutes. The purpose of these statutes is to hold accountable those who commit serious felonies for any injuries resulting from the felonies. In New York, if a person commits or attempts to commit a felony deemed particularly dangerous, such as robbery, burglary, kidnapping, arson, or forcible rape, and causes the death of a nonparticipant in the crime, he can be convicted of felony murder. His intent need not have been to cause the death; it could have been accidental. Nonetheless, he could be sentenced to life in prison for the crime.

New York and other states have felony-assault statutes based on the same principles. If a person commits a felony, thereby causing a serious physical injury to a nonparticipant, he can be convicted of first-degree assault, which in New York carries a maximum sentence of twenty-five years in prison.

---

7. *Clarke v. Brockway Motor Trucks*, D.C. Pa, 372 F.Supp. 1342 (1974).

Legislators, judges, and legal scholars have fully debated the felony-murder and felony-assault doctrines, and the consensus is that they are necessary tools to deter persons from committing felonies and to deter such persons from compounding their felonies by actions likely to lead to further injuries. It is illogical to hold that a felon can be punished when his felony results in unintended injuries to others and yet can be rewarded when he is the one injured as a consequence of his own actions.

In *People v. Hernandez and Santana*, 82 N.Y.2d 309 (1993), the defendants had robbed an undercover state police officer at gunpoint. When other officers attempted to apprehend Hernandez, he ran and then turned and pointed a gun at the officers. One officer shot at Hernandez; however, he missed and struck and killed a second police officer. Under a felony-murder charge, Hernandez and Santana were convicted and held responsible for the killing of the second officer because their actions set in motion the chain of events leading to the officer's death. It would have been nonsensical to have given Hernandez a monetary award if the first officer's bullet had hit him instead of the second officer. Hernandez, by his felonious conduct, had caused the bullet to be fired.

Like that of Hernandez, McCummings' felonious conduct caused the police to shoot. The bullet struck McCummings, rather than a third party, and he should not have been rewarded for an injury sustained during the commission of a crime.

Personal-injury lawyers will surely argue that McCummings, because of his paralysis, needed a large monetary award to pay for his care and medical expenses. It should be pointed out, however, that had McCummings not received the award, he still would have received from the government the required care and medical treatment. There was no need to create an illogical, inconsistent body of police-liability law to provide an alternative means of providing resources for severely injured citizens. The only real beneficiaries of the liability awards are the attorneys who receive the large contingency fees.

Under present conditions, as detrimental as they are, it is unlikely that the increasing number of police-liability lawsuits will be reversed. Police administrators who must deal with the current circumstances have attempted to minimize police exposure. In the wake of *Garner, McCummings*, and a host of similar cases, police administrators have reduced the authority of individual officers and have modified operational tactics in an effort to avoid exorbitant jury awards and settlements. Unfortunately, officers on the front lines still have to fight violent crime and still have to use force in many situations. Police administrators, and their legal advisors, must take measures to mitigate the results of the conflict between aggressive crime fighting and police liability. Police officers should realize they will continue to be the focus of attention and their actions will continue to be scrutinized and challenged.

Curtailing Qualified Immunity for Police

For most police-liability lawsuits, police officers can raise an affirmative defense of qualified immunity. In some areas, the defense has been expanded, but relative to the growing theories on which police can be sued, it has been curtailed. Police officers contemplating police action should not rely on this affirmative defense, since so many lawsuits are being decided on this issue, and the traditional principles of qualified immunity are changing day to day.

At common law, public officials enjoy varying degrees of immunity from lawsuits. In the criminal justice system, judges, jurors, and district attorneys have absolute immunity for discretionary decisions made in the course of their lawful duties. Were that not the case, judges and jurors would be reluctant to render a guilty verdict, and district attorneys would be reluctant to prosecute criminals. The law does not countenance such lawsuits. If a citizen files a lawsuit against a judge, juror, or district attorney for discretionary acts committed in their official capacity, the lawsuit will be dismissed. The arguments and evidence of the plaintiff will not be submitted to a jury.

The renowned jurist, Learned Hand, provided the rationale for absolute immunity for criminal justice officials.

> It does indeed go without saying than an official, who is in fact guilty of using his powers to vent his spleen upon others, or for any other personal motive not connected with the public good, should not escape liability for the injuries he may so cause; and, if it were possible in practice to confine such complaints to the guilty, it would be monstrous to deny recovery. The justification for doing so is that it is impossible to know whether the claim is well founded until the case has been tried, and that to submit all officials, the innocent as well as the guilty, to the burden of a trial and to the inevitable danger of its outcome, would dampen the ardor of all but the most resolute, or the most irresponsible, in the unflinching discharge of their duties. Again and again the public interest calls for action which may turn out to be founded on a mistake, in the face of which an official may later find himself hard put to it to satisfy a jury of his good faith. There

must indeed be means of punishing public officers who have been truant to their duties; but that is quite another matter from exposing such as have been honestly mistaken to suit by anyone who has suffered from their errors. As is so often the case, the answer must be found in a balance between the evils inevitable in either alternative. In this instance it has been thought in the end better to leave unredressed the wrongs done by dishonest officers than to subject those who try to do their duty to the constant dread of retaliation.[8]

Police officers have not been granted such absolute immunity. They have been granted a lesser, qualified immunity, which protects them from lawsuits when they perform their discretionary functions in a reasonably objective manner, when they make arrests or conduct searches in accordance with the standards of probable cause, or when they use force on the basis of a reasonable belief that such force is necessary to effect a lawful arrest, prevent escape from custody, or protect the public safety. These qualified immunities have been granted to enable police officers to perform their duties without fear of risk to their personal assets every time they make an arrest or take other police action.

Neither absolute immunity nor qualified immunity means that criminal prosecutions are precluded against public officials who violate the law with the required culpable mental state.

In civil actions, judges in the past were more willing to dismiss suits as a matter of law and not submit cases to a jury when the police could meet the standards required for qualified immunity. In the more recent past, however, because of the predilection to have questions of material fact decided by juries, all but the most frivolous police-liability cases have been submitted to juries, and the resulting adverse verdicts have in effect dissolved the traditional qualified immunity that applied to discretionary police actions.

Qualified immunity for making arrests or conducting searches is related to the standard of probable cause. Probable cause, like the reasonably objective standard, is not easy to define or understand. *Probable cause* has been defined as evidence and information that appear reliable and that disclose facts and circumstances of such collective weight and persuasiveness as to convince a person of ordinary intelligence, judgment, and experience that it is reasonably likely that a crime is being, has been, or is about to be committed and that a particular person committed it.

---

8. *Gregoire v. Biddle*, 177 F.2d 579 (1949).

This open-ended definition can be interpreted to grant broad powers to police or to second-guess and criticize police actions. In criminal law, probable cause is determined by the judge, usually at a pretrial evidentiary hearing. In a civil action, when material issues of fact are in dispute, the question of probable cause can be submitted to the jury. Once a case goes to a jury, the outcome can be irregular and surprising.

In civil-rights actions, whether the police have qualified immunity is governed by the standard of objective reasonableness. To make this determination, courts apply a two-step process: first, the court must determine whether the facts, taken in the light most favorable to the party asserting an injury, show a violation of a constitutional right; and, second, whether the constitutional right was clearly established at the time of the violation so that a reasonable officer would know that his conduct violated the Constitution.[9]

In the area of police infringement of rights, an extensive body of law has evolved. Its evolution has been marked by case-by-case decision making, conflicting rationales, and a high degree of ideological influences.

Many cases have been contradictory. For example, in *Wilson v. Layne*, 526 U.S. 603 (1999), the Supreme Court attempted to resolve one set of conflicting opinions that arose in the lower courts. In *Wilson*, the police had invited the media to "ride along" with them as they executed a search warrant in a private home. The Court instructed that qualified immunity will be denied when a police officer violates a constitutional law that had been clearly established at the time of the violation but will be granted when the alleged constitutional violation had not been clearly established by prior decisions. Applying this principle to the case, the Court held: "It is a violation of the Fourth Amendment for police to bring members of the media or other third parties into a home during the execution of a warrant when the presence of third parties in the home was not in aid of the execution of the warrant."[10] Nevertheless, despite finding a Constitutional violation, the Court held that the law was not clearly established at the time of the officer's conduct, and, therefore, qualified immunity should be granted.[11]

The *Wilson* holding established the law regarding a "ride along" and established that a police officer who commits such a violation in the future may be denied qualified immunity. However, innumerable, other potential violations may or may not have been clearly established by prior decisions, and

---

9. *Saucier v. Katz*, 533 U.S. 194 (2001).
10. *Wilson v. Layne*, 526 U.S. 603, 614.
11. Id. at 615.

police officers may or may not receive immunity for their actions, depending on the case, the court, and the judge.

Qualified immunity in use-of-force or excessive-force cases is based on the reasonable-objectiveness standard. When police-officer defendants submit evidence that they were acting in accordance with their discretionary authority, qualified immunity should be granted by the judge unless the plaintiffs can establish, by concrete facts, evidence sufficient to convince a jury that the defendants' actions were objectively unreasonable.[12] The judge should decide this on a summary-judgment motion unless there are genuine issues of material fact to be submitted to a jury.

The question whether genuine issues of material fact exist is all important. Many judges are reluctant to decide that genuine issues do not exist, even in very questionable cases.

In *Holeman v. City of New London*, 330 F. Supp. 2d 99, New London Police Officers Greg Williams and Vincent Garcia, at 4:28 a.m., while on patrol and while investigating a "prowler call," stopped a vehicle that had tinted windows and had taken a circuitous route through the high-crime neighborhood. The officers questioned the two occupants, a female driver, Ms. Smith, and a male passenger, Darrell Holeman.

An identification check disclosed that Holeman was on parole for a narcotics felony. According to Officer Garcia, he attempted to pat down Holeman, who was uncooperative and aggressive. Holeman said, "I'll show you what I got in my pocket" and moved his hand toward his pocket. A struggle ensued, during which, according to Officer Garcia, Holeman drew a small silver handgun and pointed it at Officer Williams. Garcia shot Holeman three times. Even though Holeman was shot, Officer Williams had to strike him several times in his attempt to subdue him, and the officers used their police dog to induce Holeman to submit to handcuffs.

The officers radioed for an ambulance, which arrived within minutes. While tending to Holeman, paramedics found a small silver handgun next to the right rear tire of the vehicle, between the tire and the curb. The paramedics testified that Holeman was uncooperative and combative, and although handcuffed, he had to be strapped to a board to restrain him from injuring himself or others. Holeman was transported to the hospital, where he died shortly thereafter.

The administrators of Holeman's estate, acting as plaintiffs, sued the police for constitutional violations regarding the traffic stop, the attempted pat-

12. *Anderson v. Liberty Lobby, Inc.*, 477 U.S. 242 (1986).

down, and the use of force. The defendants moved for summary judgment, claiming qualified immunity. The trial judge denied the motion and ruled that there were genuine issues of material fact requiring a jury trial. The plaintiffs, who were not witnesses and had no concrete evidence, claimed the police planted the gun. Their basis for the claim was that the two officers could not find the gun immediately after the shooting and that the officers had time to plant the gun. Additionally, despite the deposition testimony of Smith, the female driver, that Holeman had been uncooperative and aggressive, plaintiffs claimed that he complied with the police directions and was not uncooperative and aggressive.

Plaintiffs contended that a genuine issue of material fact existed because the accounts of the two police officers differed. It would be unusual and suspicious if the two accounts were exactly the same. The officers viewed the incident from separate perspectives and were physically involved in a tense, uncertain, and rapidly evolving situation. What they observed and what they remembered would naturally differ to some degree.

The trial court summarized the evidence and the contentions:

> Garcia released his hold on Holeman when Nero (the police dog) attacked. It is not clear why Garcia stepped away from Holeman, though he may have tripped over Nero. Plaintiffs allege that Garcia drew his weapon as he stepped back from Holeman. Garcia says that he stepped back, observed Holeman pull out a silver pistol, and then drew his weapon. Witness Consuelo Rodriguez also says that she saw Holeman holding a gun. While the parties agree Garcia yells, "he's got a gun," plaintiffs deny that Holeman possessed a gun the night in question. Plaintiffs argue that, after the shooting, Williams and Garcia initially could not find the gun and had time to plant a weapon when they were alone with Holeman. The Report of the State's Attorney found that "the pistol was forensically examined for fingerprints," and "no identifiable latent impressions were developed or found."

> Defendants offer a different version of the events as they assert that Holeman possessed a gun throughout his encounter with the officers. Williams contends that he felt a metal object during the struggle and heard Garcia say that Holeman had a gun. Furthermore, Williams says that he pushed away from Holeman after hearing Garcia's shouts. Garcia testifies that he fired his weapon because he saw Holeman point the gun at Williams' head. Garcia's shot hit Holeman. At this

time, Williams, who also was wounded by Garcia's shot, fell to the ground and took cover behind the front of Smith's car. Garcia contends that he then fired two more shots because Holeman pointed the gun at him.

Either version of the events provided by the officers should have established their qualified immunity. In both versions, Holeman resisted and had a gun. The plaintiffs' contention that the police planted the gun was not based on supporting evidence. To override a qualified immunity, the plaintiffs should have had to provide some concrete evidence to support their allegations.

Moreover, any experienced fingerprint expert could have told the court that identifiable fingerprints are rarely found on the surface of a gun and the fact that no fingerprints were identifiable did not mean that Holeman did not have the gun.

The decision of the court meant that these officers might have to undergo a trial for their actions, and if this case is the standard for denying qualified immunity and sending a case to trial, then almost any police shooting will have to go to trial. Police officers should expect that they will be subjected to a lawsuit for any shooting or other case in which they use a substantial amount of force. They should prepare themselves by learning about the process and train themselves to respond to the tactics by which plaintiff attorneys will attempt to undermine their credibility and establish their liability.

CHAPTER FOUR

Tactics Used by Attorneys to Undermine and Manipulate Police Witnesses

"It would be a very good thing if every trick could receive some short and obviously appropriate name, so that when anyone used this or that particular trick, he could at once be reproved for it."

Arthur Schopenhauer: *The World as Will and Idea (1818).*

The legal profession has developed a repertoire of well-known tactics for cross-examining witnesses. Tactics for trial are substantially different from those used during a deposition. The public knows many of the trial tactics through books, television, and movies. Deposition tactics are not as well known, because no one makes movies about depositions, as they are long and tedious procedures. The following materials describe recognized deposition tactics used by attorneys, with examples adapted from actual case transcripts.

Fatigue

Depositions can last as long as seven hours per day, excluding lunch and breaks. The examining attorney will attempt to tire the witness with a volume of questions, a repetition of questions in varying forms, and minutiae. The attorney does this for a living and is better prepared than the witness to stay focused and sharp throughout the process. A deposition is like a marathon. Staying power determines who wins in the end, and most witnesses will tire long before the attorney. Under a constant barrage of questions, hour after hour, a witness can become impatient, lose concentration, and at some point, just to get the ordeal over, begin to concede answers the attorney wants.

In federal court, depositions are generally limited to one day. In state courts, no written rules limit the number of days that can be taken with a witness. In the O.J. Simpson civil case in California, Simpson was deposed for eleven days. But with rare exceptions, the attorney will want to finish the deposition of a witness within one day. The attorney does not want to give the witness a break to go home, rest, and prepare.

Occasionally during especially long depositions, one or both attorneys will exhibit signs of stress. In a New York case in which a police officer's deposition had gone on for several hours, the officer's counsel objected.

Q. Do you have any document in front of you that would refresh your recollection?

A. No.

Examining Attorney: I'll ask that a search be conducted, and to the extent that there are additional reports, that they be identified.

Witness' Counsel: I strongly object. Ask the plaintiff if she filed any other reports. Ask her to put it on a paper, on an affidavit, and we'll do a search. I'm not going on a wild goose chase and start searching the records again after we have all the records in front of us. My police officer is saying this is the whole file.

Examining Attorney: Off the record.

Witness' Counsel: No, no, on the record.

Examining Attorney: We are just cluttering the record.

Witness' Counsel: No, I'm not cluttering the record. I'm putting a statement on the record. If you don't want to pay for this part, I'll pay for it, my God. It is clear. You have my witness. She's been here all day. She's tired. You're trying to get blood from a stone right now, counsel, and that's a problem, and I think soon—I mean, you have to call the Judge. This is a problem, and I can't subject my witness to this. This is a long, long deposition.

The examining counsel said that the objection was noted, then proceeded to ask questions for several more hours.

Getting the Witness to Talk

The attorney will not tip his hand by letting the witness know that the deposition may last hours. In fact, he may foster the impression that the deposition will not take long. He may begin with a casual, friendly approach, using mild flattery or humor in an attempt to relax the witness and get him off guard.

The attorney will ask about the witness' personal background, prior employment, and education. With police officers, he will ask simple questions about police work that will allow the officer to show his specialized knowledge. He may play dumb and ask the officer for an explanation of police jargon.

Low-key Approach

The attorney may ask questions as though the answers are not important or are just a side matter. He may say, "By the way," or "Before we proceed," or "I just want to clarify something that I was a little confused about." Or he may give the witness the impression that his answers are not expected to be exact. He may say, "I know it's been a long time since the incident, so you may not remember exactly all the details, but tell us what you can remember."

Combative Approach

Diametrically opposed to the low-key approach is the combative approach. Some attorneys will attempt to anger or bully the witness by adopting an accusatory attitude or will attempt to unnerve and put the witness on the defensive by asking demeaning questions. They may ask a police officer, "Were you ever convicted of a felony?" "Do you take drugs?" "Were you ever suspended from duty?" "Ever investigated by the Internal Affairs Bureau?" "Ever the subject of civilian complaints?" If the officer answers affirmatively, they will ask what the charges or allegations were.

Some attorneys will challenge an officer's truthfulness. "Officer, do you really expect us to believe that?" "Come on, officer, let's not insult our intelligence here."

Police officers are particularly susceptible to these kinds of tactics. They are accustomed to being the ones in control. When they unexpectedly find themselves in an adversarial situation in which their integrity is blatantly challenged or demeaned, some officers react emotionally, lose concentration, and fail to focus properly on the questions and answers.

In the event an attorney finds a weakness in an officer's answers, he will hammer on the point of weakness. In a Queens, New York, suicide-by-cop case, the police had been called to a family dispute in which the plaintiff allegedly had assaulted his ex-wife. When the police arrived, the plaintiff answered the door, took a combat stance, pointed a black object at an officer, and said he was going to kill the officer. The officer shot and wounded the plaintiff. The black object turned out to be a cell phone.

The plaintiff was charged with assaulting his ex-wife, but the police did not charge him with any crime in relation to the officer. Subsequently, the charge of assaulting the ex-wife was dismissed. The plaintiff then sued the police in federal court for false arrest, false imprisonment, excessive use of force, malicious prosecution, and violation of constitutional rights.

During the officer's deposition, the attorney questioned him regarding his failure to charge the plaintiff with a crime committed against the officer.

Q. Did you understand what he was being arrested for?

A. Menacing.

Q. As you sit here today, are you able to articulate to me what you understand as a police officer to be the elements of the crime of menacing?

A. If I was to take the stapler and raise it like I was going to hit you.

Q. That would be menacing?

A. Or make pretend I was going to throw it. Yes.

Q. Other than to give me an example, are you able to articulate the elements? In other words, for example, I would say a misdemeanor assault would involve unwanted touching of another person with the intent to cause physical injury and the causing of serious physical injury. So in that regard, are you able, from your training as a police officer, able to articulate your understand of what elements of menacing are?

Witness' Counsel: Objection. I'll note that that's incorrect. Misdemeanor assault is not serious physical injury.

A. No.

Q. Are you able to articulate that?

A. I don't know what degrees, no.

Q. And did you ever tell anyone that the plaintiff had engaged in the crime of menacing?

A. I don't recall.

Q. Did you ever tell anyone that the plaintiff should be charged with menacing?

A. Don't recall.

Q. Did you ever have an understanding at any time, up to the present day as you sit her right now, as to whether the plaintiff was charged with menacing or not?

A. Don't recall.

Q. Did you become aware that he was charged with something?

A. Yes.

Q. How did you become aware of that?

A. In the news, newspapers.

Q. What did you hear in the news?

A. That he beat his wife.

Q. Did you ever speak to anybody in the District Attorney's Office about the charges against the plaintiff?

A. Don't recall.

Q. Why weren't you made the arresting officer?

A. He was arrested on other charges.

Q. Well, you told me he was arrested for menacing, right?

A. I don't know what they put down.

Q. Well, you say you witnessed the plaintiff commit the crime of menacing?

A. Correct.

Q. Why weren't you made the arresting officer then?

A. It's not always the way it works.

Q. What do you mean by that?

A. We were removed from the scene. Further investigation was done.

Q. So some officer in a supervisory role, he may determine to make somebody else the arresting officer, correct?

A. Correct.

Q. And then it's important for an officer who may have witnessed something that the arresting officer didn't witness, to be able to give his input so all possible charges can be brought, correct?

A. Could be possible.

Q. And you knew you had witnessed the plaintiff, according to you, commit the crime of menacing, and that no one else had witnessed that, except your partner, correct, no other police people?

A. Correct.

Q. And did you ever attempt to go speak to the arresting officer and let him know what you had witnessed?

A. No.

Q. Why not?

A. It was investigated by someone else.

Q. Didn't you feel it was important that the plaintiff be charged with the crime of menacing?

A. I really didn't know what was charged.

Q. I'm not asking you what you know he was charged with, I'm asking you whether or not you felt it was important that he be charged, regardless of other charges, with the crime of menacing, which you say you have witnessed?

A. It wasn't the first thing that came to mind, no.

Q. Did you want him to be charged with menacing?

A. I don't recall.

Q. Well, would you agree that as a police officer, part of your job is to effect arrests of people for who you believe there's probable cause to arrest?

A. Yes.

Q. And in this case, it's your testimony that you observed a crime being committed, right?

A. Correct.

Q. Did you ever speak to anyone about observing the plaintiff commit the crime of menacing as you say?

A. I don't recall.

Q. Did you become aware that he went to trial in criminal court at some point on the charge that was brought against him?

A. I don't recall.

Q. You knew that he was arrested and charged in criminal court, right?

A. Correct.

Q. You're not sure what he was charged with; is that correct?

A. Correct.

Q. Do you know what the outcome of the charges were?

A. No.

Q. As you sit here today, do you know what the outcome was?

A. No.

Q. So if I told you he was acquitted of misdemeanor assault, you don't know whether that happened or not.

A. No.

Q. Would you agree that if the plaintiff was charged with menacing, for him to be convicted, either you or your partner would have had to testify?

A. It's possible.

Q. And did you ever seek to find out if the DA's office was charging him with menacing so you could make sure that you would be called to testify against him?

A. I don't recall.

The plaintiff's attorney engaged in this kind of questioning for several hours before turning to questions about the facts of the physical confrontation, and by that time the officer had been substantially worn down and placed on the defensive.

Avoiding the Main Issue

The attorney may start with a subject the witness is not expecting. This tactic catches a witness off guard and prevents the witness from beginning with prepared answers. He may ask about the witness' prior employment, his police training, or about courses and instructions in the police academy. He may go over every movement leading up to the main incident, asking obvious questions, such as: Did you get into the police car? Did you drive toward the location? Did you make a left turn at the corner? Did you park the car? Did you get out of the car?

The attorney may ask about the police manual, regulations, and procedures. If related to the case, he may ask legal questions about probable cause or the standards for the use of deadly physical force. He can test the witness' knowledge. If the witness is not doing well, the attorney prolongs the questioning. When he can, he will sow seeds of doubt in the witness. By the time the attorney gets to the main issues of the case, the witness is less certain of his position and knowledge. The witness, in order to remain consistent with prior answers, may have to alter his position and concede points and possibilities.

Switching from Subject to Subject

The attorney can switch from subject to subject in order to disrupt or confuse a witness. At a trial, the attorney has to consider the judge and the jury.

He needs to present a line of questioning that can be followed. A judge will not allow irrelevant or confusing questions. At a deposition, however, the attorney is not constrained by those considerations and can purposefully confuse the deposition witness in order to extract admissions, contradictions, and other damaging answers.

A disadvantage to this approach for the attorney is that the transcript of the deposition may be less than coherent and will be difficult to follow in front of a jury at a trial; nevertheless, the advantages of keeping a witness off balance may outweigh the disadvantages, and many attorneys employ the switching around tactic.

Mixing Up the Chronology of the Event

The attorney knows that prior to the deposition the officer may have prepared a chronological narrative of what occurred. If allowed to recite his narrative, the officer could do so with confidence and clarity. The attorney will attempt to avoid the prepared narrative and disrupt the officer's train of thought by changing the time-line and asking questions out of sequence.

When the officer attempts to recite his narrative, the attorney will interrupt the flow. Just as the witness is getting to the main points, the attorney will switch to some other subject. It can be something minor and insignificant but enough to distract the witness' attention. The attorney may never return to that portion of the narrative or may return to the narrative at a different point or from a different angle.

An example of this type of interruption occurred in the case of a police shooting of a suspect in Suffolk County, New York. Two officers spotted a vehicle that fit the description of a vehicle used in a robbery and a shooting. They pulled their unmarked police car in front of the suspect vehicle, which was parked in a driveway. The male suspect and his female companion were seated in the front seat of the car. The officers ordered the male to get out of the car with his hands up. The suspect did so, but did not immediately put his hands up. His hands were down inside the front of his pants. One of the officers, believing the suspect had a gun, shot him. A subsequent search of the suspect revealed he was not carrying a gun.

At the officer's deposition, he attempted to explain his actions, but was interrupted in the flow of his narrative by the examining attorney.

Q. When you observed him getting out of his vehicle, can you describe how he did it?

A. I was yelling "Police. Don't Move. Police don't move."

At that time the door had opened. Plaintiff was getting out. I could not see his hands. I began to scream "Let me see your hands." As he cleared the door of his vehicle, that's when I observed where his hands were. His hands were buried down in front of his pants in the area of his waistband, and there was a bulge. At that point....

Q. The rest of the story, we will get to that. When you observed plaintiff getting out of the vehicle, were you already out of your vehicle?

A. Yes.

Q. When you observed the door, the passenger door on the side where plaintiff was, did you observe that door actually opening?

A. Yes.

By the above maneuver, the attorney gained control of the testimony. He prevented the officer from giving his uninterrupted version of the event and reduced the officer to giving yes or no answers to the attorney's presentation of the event.

Questions Designed to Manipulate Witnesses

Many attorneys conduct depositions in a fair, straightforward way. They stick to the chronology of the event and ask the witness what occurred next, and their follow-up questions are based on the answers given by the witness. However, some attorneys will resort to the unethical practice of asking questions that assume facts not in evidence or that mischaracterize prior testimony. This is done to induce a witness to accept the attorney's premise for a question. Counsel for the witness should anticipate such practices and object to their use. Sometimes the counsel may not, so the witness must also be on guard for such questions and should ask for clarification. When an examining attorney attempts to paraphrase prior testimony, the witness should be alert for discrepancies.

Leading, compound, and forced-choice questions on direct deposition examination are often used to manipulate witnesses.

Leading questions have been defined as:

1. Questions that call for only a "yes" or "no" answer.
2. Questions that are framed to suggest the desired answer.

3.   Questions that assume the facts in controversy.

Many leading questions end with the phrase, "Is that correct?" Or, "Is that right?" Or, "Is that a fair statement?" Others reverse the order, for example: "Isn't it true that while you were with the defendant, he told you that he was going to kill his wife?"

A leading question puts words into a witness' mouth that are to be echoed back or plainly suggests the answer that the attorney wishes to get from the witness. A witness may unconsciously accept the suggestion of a question, and the attorney may, by the use of leading questions, supply a false memory for the witness or suggest desired answers that are not based upon real recollection.[1]

The advantage of leading questions is that the attorney keeps control of the witness. A leading question is most often a statement by the attorney to which he asks the witness to agree. If the question/statement is 90 to 99 percent accurate, a witness, especially a tired, beaten-down witness, may tend to agree. If a witness is not careful when answering such questions, he may find that he has been manipulated into giving answers that are adverse to his position or his true recollection of the event.

Witnesses need to be on guard for these questions. If the question is not accurate, the witness should say, "No" or "That's not correct."

Under our rules of legal procedure and evidence, leading questions are properly used for cross-examinations during a trial. They should not be used for direct examination by an attorney who calls a witness to the stand, although there are exceptions for setting the stage, clarifications, or for a hostile witness.

By statute, depositions are to follow the same questioning procedures and rules applicable to trials, therefore, an attorney deposing a witness, even an adversary, should not lead the witness.[2] Nevertheless, leading questions are frequently asked, and although they may be stricken from the record at a later time, the witness is still subjected to them. Since a judge is not present at a deposition, attorneys have more leeway with leading or other objectionable questions.

In a Queens, New York, case, an attorney filed a lawsuit against the New York City Police Department in which he alleged that the police injured an

---

1. Jerome Prince, *Richardson on Evidence*, 10th ed. (New York: Brooklyn Law School, 1973) Section 478.

2. *NY Civil Practice Law and Rules*, Section 3113.

eight-month-old baby. He alleged the police did this by shaking the baby and throwing the baby to the floor in order to coerce the plaintiff, the baby's father, into giving them information about a triple homicide. During depositions, the attorney attempted to manipulate the police officers involved into giving answers that he could use to build a circumstantial case against them.

The police had received information that the murder weapon had been sold by the plaintiff, who was known to sell illegal firearms. As part of the investigation, a confidential informant entered the plaintiff's apartment and purchased illegal guns from him. The plaintiff's wife was present in the apartment when the sale was made. Based on the illegal sale, the police obtained a search warrant for the plaintiff's apartment. Their plan was to arrest the suspect and to question him to find out whether he could provide information about the gun used in the murders or the whereabouts of the perpetrator.

When the police entered the apartment to execute the search warrant, seven people were in the apartment, including the plaintiff, his wife, their two children, two other women and one other male. One child was a toddler, the other was the eight-month-old boy. As the police searched the apartment, three officers attempted to question the plaintiff, but he did not provide any information. The plaintiff, his wife, and the other adult occupants of the apartment were arrested, and, in accordance with procedures, a policewoman took custody of the children and transported them to a children's shelter.

The next day, the children were transferred from the shelter to a foster home. One day later, the foster parent took the baby to a hospital because the baby repeatedly threw himself backwards, would not eat, constantly cried, and vomited. At the hospital, the baby was diagnosed as having shaken-baby syndrome, internal brain bleeding and no external injuries. After treatment and release from the hospital, the baby was placed with new foster parents, who also had to take the baby to the hospital after he had repeatedly struck his head on the crib railing.

Between the time of the arrests and the baby's first hospitalization, neither the plaintiff nor his wife had made any complaints alleging that the police shook or injured the baby. Ten days after the first hospitalization, the plaintiff made a complaint to the NYPD Internal Affairs Bureau in which he alleged the police injured the baby.

A month later, the plaintiff was re-interviewed by the Internal Affairs Bureau investigators, and he recanted his initial accusations. He stated that there were no injuries to his son, and the police did not shake or throw the baby against the wall. Soon thereafter, he pled guilty to sale and possession of unlawful firearms and to endangering the welfare of a child. Despite his recantation, he filed a lawsuit against the police, repeating the original allegations.

Three years later, his attorney began taking depositions of the police officers who had executed the search warrant. Apparently, the attorney's tactic was to establish that the police were angry at the plaintiff for his failure to cooperate with their investigation, and this anger motivated them to engage in the egregious misconduct. His tactic was also to establish that two officers, a sergeant and a detective, were in close proximity to the plaintiff and the baby, and they could have held the baby in front of the plaintiff and threatened to injure the baby. The attorney asked the police lieutenant who had been in charge of executing the search warrant the following questions:

Q. He (the plaintiff) was uncooperative?

A. In my eyes, yes.

Q. Is it because you believe that he was withholding information that he, in fact, had?

A. Yes.

Q. During the questioning of the (plaintiff), would it be fair to say that you, yourself, were within his personal space.

At this point, the witness' counsel objected to the leading question that supplied the phrase "personal space," and the witness did not answer. The witness' counsel did an excellent job throughout the depositions in thwarting many of the inappropriate efforts of the examining attorney.

Q. How close were you in proximity, physically, when you were questioning him?

A. Two, three feet.

Q. How about the sergeant, how close was he?

A. Everybody was about the same distance.

Q. How about the detective?

A. About two to three feet.

Q. Would it be fair to say that the three members of the police force, you, the sergeant and the detective, were encircling the main subject?

The witness' counsel objected to the leading question that suggested "encircling," and the witness did not answer.

Q. At any time while you were inside the apartment, did you ever take your eyes off the baby?

A. Yes.

Q. At any time while you were inside the apartment, did you ever take your eyes off the detective?

A. Yes.

Q. Was there any time that were inside the apartment that you did not see the detective?

A. Yes.

Q. How many times would you say that you did not see the detective?

A. I cannot give you an exact.

Q. Would it be more than five minutes?

A. No.

Q. Would it be less than five minutes?

A. Yes.

Q. While you were in the apartment, was there any time that you did not see the sergeant?

A. Yes.

Q. How much time was that?

A. Several minutes.

Q. Was it the same time that you did not see the detective?

A. Yes.

Q. How many times did you take your eyes off the sergeant?

A. I would say a couple again.

Q. During the time that you were in the apartment, what was the total length of time that you did not observe the sergeant?

A. Three, four, five minutes.

Q. During those three or four, five minutes, were you in different locations throughout the apartment or in the same location in the apartment?

A. Very small apartment. I mean, I might—I don't know exactly where I was.

At this point in the deposition, the examining attorney through leading questions, and, perhaps, by confusing the witness, had converted a number of "times" that the lieutenant took his eyes off the detective into one single stretch of several minutes in which he did not see either the detective or the sergeant. If not refuted, the attorney could have established the "window of opportunity" for the shaking of the baby to have occurred, which could be extremely useful for development before a jury. The attorney could imply to the jury that the detective or the sergeant, or both, shook the baby when the lieutenant did not see them.

When the attorney took the deposition of the policewoman who had taken the baby from the apartment to the shelter, he attempted to lead the policewoman into providing testimony that would further this theory. However, the policewoman's counsel was alert to the tactics and continued to object to inappropriate questions.

Q. You left the apartment at that point?

A. Yeah. We were leaving the apartment at that point, and that's when the newborn baby, the brother, was handed to me at that point.

Q. When you say, "We were leaving the apartment," who do you mean by that?

A. It was me and Detective Blank.

Q. Prior to that point, what was Detective Blank doing?

A. I don't recall.

Q. Do you know the name of the officer that handed you the baby?

A. I don't recall.

At this point, the witness' counsel objected to the question that assumed that an officer handed her the baby, rather than the mother or one of the other civilians in the apartment.

Q. You said somebody handed you the baby?

A. Correct.

Q. Was it a member of the New York City Police Department that handed you the baby?

A. I don't recall.

The questioning shifted to other issues, and after several minutes of questioning the attorney again asked a leading question, which assumed testimony not in evidence that an officer handed the baby to the policewoman.

Q. Did you see any police officers shake the baby?

A. No.

Q. Did you see any police officers injure the baby?

A. No.

Q. Aside from the officer that handed the baby to you and yourself, did any other members of the New York City Police Department hold the baby?

A. I don't know.

Again, the witness' counsel objected to the question that an officer handed the baby to her. The successful resistance to the plaintiff attorney's leading questions played an important part in thwarting his intentions.

Compound Questions

Compound questions can lead to ambiguous answers. There are generally two kinds: the "and" construction or the "or" construction. The following is a simple "and" construction.

Question: "Did you drive through a stop sign and down a one-way street?"

If the witness did only one of the above, he could truthfully answer, "No." Of course, it might be taken to mean a denial of both, and if one can be proved, the witness might be made to look as if he had lied.

The best method is to ask for clarification or answer both parts.

The following is a simple "or" construction.

Question: "At the point of the river where he fell in, was the current slow or swift?"

Either characterization, "swift" or "slow," could be inaccurate. If they were both inaccurate, the witness should not be compelled to adopt either.

Forced-choice Questions

Forced-choice questions are also leading, for example: "Did you approach the plaintiff from the front or from the back?"

The answer may be neither. A witness should not accept inaccurate choices or the setup described by the attorney. Forced-choice questions can be confusing and can trick an officer into giving an inaccurate or unnecessary answer. In one lawsuit alleging unnecessary force by police, the following exchange took place during the deposition of a police officer.

Q: Was the sergeant behind the plaintiff trying to reach over to bring his hands down or was he face to face in front of him?

A: I don't believe they were face to face but they were across from each other. The sergeant grabbed him by the arms.

A truthful answer, but unnecessary. The question led to two choices, neither of which might have been exactly accurate. The officer tried to explain what happened and, in doing so, added information. He could have said, "I wouldn't describe it in either of the ways you described it."

The attorney would be compelled to ask, "Okay, how would you describe it?"

Now the officer could use his own words and his own narrative. By refusing to subscribe to the attorney's setup, the officer retains control of his answers.

When the attorney insists on a yes or no answer, the officer should only do so if the premise of the question is accurate.

Questions about Conversations

Witness testimony about physical facts and actions observed is the primary evidence used to reconstruct an event. Nonetheless, in almost all police-liability cases, the legal conclusions drawn about an incident must also take into account the state of mind of the participants in the incident. When a police officer fires his gun at a person, it is important to know what the officer was thinking when he fired. It is important to know whether the officer fired out of a genuine and reasonable fear for his own safety or for some other reason, such as anger at the person for not complying with his orders.

To ascertain or infer a participant's state of mind, attorneys will ask what words were uttered before, during, and after the incident. They will ask what other persons said to the participant and how the participant reacted. At the trial, hearsay issues may be raised by such questions; nevertheless, at the deposition, they will be allowed.

Questions Designed to Imply a Cover-up

A favorite tactic is to develop a claim of police cover-up, invoking the "blue wall of silence," which is the idea that police will always lie to cover up the mistakes or wrongdoing of brother officers. To establish the existence of a blue wall of silence, attorneys delve into the conversations or lack of conversations between police officers. The purpose is to determine whether the attorney can paint a picture for the jury of a group of police officers conspiring to concoct a story and to cover up the facts. Attorneys who sue police know juries are receptive to the idea of a cover-up. It is what they have seen on television and in the movies, and they believe it.

Undoubtedly, the attorney will ask, "Officer, at any time between the time of the incident and before you came here to court today, did you discuss the facts of the case with your partner or any of your brother officers?"

If the officer admits to having conversations, but is evasive or vague about the content, the attorney might be able to imply that these conversations were designed to concoct a story. If the officer denies any such conversations, the attorney will attempt to show that it is unrealistic and not credible for officers to refrain from talking about a serious incident, such as a shooting or use of other physical force. The attorney will use either the evasive answers or the denials to paint a picture of a police conspiracy.

In the event that the officer states that he had discussions with other officers, the attorney will question him about what was said, which can open up theoretical areas of inquiry. Conversations can be interpreted in different ways, with dissimilar conclusions drawn from them. Since everyone perceives and interprets observations individually, contradictions invariably arise, and a shrewd attorney can use these contradictions to undermine police credibility. An attorney will ask what an officer meant by a statement or what did the officer think was meant by the statement of another. This type of non-concrete evidence is the material from which an attorney can create the perception that a blue wall of silence actually exists.

In *Busch vs. City of New York*,[3] tried in the U.S. District Court, Eastern District of New York, the attorney for the plaintiff attempted to use the officers' denials that they talked among themselves about the case to attack their credibility. The case involved Gary Busch, apparently a mentally disturbed man, who allegedly lunged at several police officers with a raised hammer in his hand. Four of the officers shot him, hitting him twelve times. His family sued for wrongful death and violation of his constitutional rights, and the trial was held in November 2003.

As reported in the *New York Times*, Busch's attorney called the officers to the witness stand and questioned them with the intention of showing the jury that the officers "fabricated an account that would portray Mr. Busch as more threatening than he was."[4]

The officers testified that even though they were together for several hours at the hospital and at the station house after the shooting, they had not discussed the events at that time or at any other time during the years leading

---

3. *Busch v. City of New York*, US District Court, EDNY, 00 Civ. 5211, 2003.
4. William Glaberson, "Retracing Their Words," *New York Times*, November 2, 2003.

up to the trial. "The officers insisted that they had not discussed the shooting among themselves.... They did not ask one another who had fired and who had not."[5]

Plaintiff's attorney "was clearly counting on the jurors to conclude that it was unlikely that the officers did not talk about what happened, as their adrenaline pumped and an inevitable, painful investigation geared up with the potential to ruin careers and, perhaps, lives."[6]

Whether the officers ever talked about the case was disputed; however, it would probably have been better if they had done so, and if they had admitted to talking about it. Discussions and questions are perfectly normal. Most juries would expect that officers would ask simple questions such as, "Did you fire?" Or, "How many shots did you fire?" Or, "When did you fire?" To deny any conversations at all lends itself to insinuations about the proverbial "blue wall of silence."

A testifying officer is in a dilemma because he knows that if he answers affirmatively that discussions occurred, the attorney will delve into what was said. The officer, mindful of the rubric not to volunteer information and not to open himself up to an allegation of collusion, often will give an ambiguous answer. Something like, "Well, he asked me if I was okay. And I asked him, if he was okay. But we never really got into the details."

The attorney will follow up sarcastically. "Oh, you never discussed whether the plaintiff had a gun or not? You never got together to make sure your stories matched? Come on, officer. Do you expect the jury to believe that?"

In the Busch case, after an exceptionally contentious trial, the jury found that the officers were not liable for violating Busch's constitutional rights. However, the plaintiff made a motion to the trial judge to set aside the jury verdict because of the disputed evidence. The trial judge did so, and ordered a new trial for the violation of the Fourth Amendment by the use of excessive force. In his memorandum explaining his order, the judge, among other issues, pointed to testimony that contradicted the police officers' position that they did not confer and collude after the shooting. He wrote:

> Allegations of collusion by both parties permeated this trial. Plaintiff proffered testimony that the officers discussed the shooting at the scene of the shooting and afterward.... A civilian witness, testified that while at Maimonides Hospital, he saw three officers enter

---

5. Ibid.
6. Ibid.

together. He testified that one officer was "slugged over to the right slightly and he was like: Oh, what did I do? And he was going: Oh, what did I do, what did I do?" ... (The witness) testified that he saw another officer grab that officer, pull him into a room and shush him in order to keep him quiet.... Lastly..., a Fire Department paramedic who worked per diem as a hospital paramedic, testified that the officers were talking with one another in a group within a thirty foot circle after the shooting.[7]

Although the judge's ruling did not cite evidence of what the officers said to one another about the shooting, the fact that they denied any discussions raised a negative inference against them. The fundamental legal concept— false in one, false in all—was applied, and the loss of credibility for the officers in this relatively immaterial matter affected their credibility regarding the actual circumstances of the shooting.

Questions about Conversations with Counsel

Despite the attorney-client privilege, an examining attorney may ask a witness, "Have you discussed this case with your attorney?" He may ask how many times, where and when, and who was present. Attorney-client conversations, to be privileged, must be confidential. If other persons were present during the conversations, the privilege may have been lost. If lost, the examining attorney may attempt to ascertain what was said in the conversations.

Another controversial issue is whether the witness and his counsel may confer during breaks in the deposition. Courts have rendered differing opinions. It is settled that during a break counsel cannot coach a witness about the substance of his testimony, and the discussion during that coaching would not be covered by the attorney-client privilege. In some instances, exceptions apply to correct inadvertent mistakes or to discuss privileges.

After a break, the examining attorney may ask the witness about such conversations, and the witness, depending on the circumstances, may have to answer.

---

7. *Busch v. City of New York*, supra, Memorandum and Order, Hon. Sterling Johnson, 2004, 21.

Prior Inconsistent Statements

As a police-liability case progresses toward trial, several thresholds are passed, and the cut-and-dried cases are dismissed or settled. It is the border-line cases, those that can be interpreted differently and argued from both sides that proceed to the deposition stage. Usually two conflicting versions of the incident will have developed: the police version, which purports that the police acted lawfully within the scope of their duties, reasonably, and in accordance with the proper standards of police conduct; and the plaintiff's version, which contends that the police acted unlawfully in violation of their duties, unreasonably, unnecessarily, and either negligently or willfully in a wrongful manner.

The legal purpose of a deposition is to obtain information to reconstruct a truthful and accurate account of the incident. At the deposition stage, the plaintiff attorney seeks to obtain information that will support his version of the incident and will undermine the police version. The facts of the incident are not going to change, but the statements about the facts can change, and the credibility of a police-officer witness can be destroyed.

The attorney may have copies of prior statements, including but not limited to statements the officer made in the course of filing criminal charges against the plaintiff; transcripts of testimony the officer gave at criminal court hearings, grand jury proceedings, or at a trial; audio tapes of statements the officer made during police department administrative investigations; applications for commendations in connection with the incident; or reports of injuries suffered during the incident.

In order to uncover inconsistencies, the attorney will not show the witness his prior statements but will first obtain a new account from the witness. He may then confront the witness with any prior inconsistencies or he may reserve the information for use at trial.

The police-officer witness may realize at deposition that a number of discrepancies have been demonstrated, but he may assume that it is entirely natural for a certain number of discrepancies to exist in any account of an incident. He may believe the discrepancies do not amount to much, but at trial he may find that the attorney has collected all the discrepancies and presented them to the jury in a way that paints a portrait of an incompetent or lying police officer. Then, before deliberations, the judge will instruct the jury that if they believe a witness lied about one thing, they may conclude that he lied about everything.

Discrepancies and Omissions in Written Reports

Writing reports of crimes, accidents, injuries, and arrests are a routine and integral part of the police function. Nevertheless, officers, for a variety of reasons, may prepare these reports in a cursory or less than perfect manner. After making an arrest, for example, an officer must process and take his prisoner to court within a limited time frame. Pressed for time and not contemplating that the arrest will become the subject of a lawsuit, an officer may commit errors or omissions when filling out forms and may include only the minimal requirements for the report to be accepted for processing.

At the deposition, after eliciting narrative testimony from the officer, which quite frequently will have differences from the original reports of the incident, the plaintiff attorney will lead the officer to testify that he or she had been trained and had a duty to prepare reports accurately. He will lead the officer to testify that he always did his duty to the best of his ability and would never purposefully put inaccurate or misleading information in an official police department report. Then the attorney will confront the officer with the reports in question and make the officer explain any omissions, errors, or discrepancies. The officer will be in the position of having to disavow either his current testimony or his reports.

The following is a composite example from a deposition in which the detective witness apparently had failed to review reports he had prepared. At first, the detective denied any recollection of the incident, but the plaintiff's attorney, using the reports, was able to discredit the detective's denial and to establish the essential facts necessary to prove his case against the police department.

The plaintiff had been arrested for murder, served a year in jail, and was released when the district attorney dismissed the case.

The plaintiff sued the police department for false arrest, malicious prosecution, and violation of civil rights. He contended that he had been arrested in order to pressure his brother into confessing to the murder. He claimed he was arrested without probable cause and that the police fabricated evidence that an eyewitness had pointed him out as he walked into the police station.

The lawsuit took some time to proceed, and ten years after the arrest, the detective was deposed. At first, he testified that he was not the lead investigator and did not have an independent recollection of the arrest. The attorney pressured him for information, but the detective resisted. The following are extracts from the deposition:

Q. Do you recall specifically any involvement in an investigation involving the homicide of an individual named Jones?

A. Not particularly, no, sir.

Q. As you sit here today, do you have any independent recollection of either the murder or that investigation?

A. Only the paperwork I reviewed with counsel. That is all I recall.

Q. Did that paperwork that you reviewed with counsel refresh your recollection in any way?

A. Actually, no, sir.

Q. Based upon your review of the materials that you looked at with counsel prior to today's deposition, is it your understanding that the arrest of the plaintiff was based on the use of confidential informants?

A. I don't know if I necessarily agree with that.

Q. Based on your independent recollection and what you have read to refresh your recollection, what do you understand is the basis for the arrest of plaintiff for murder?

A. I don't think I follow your question.

Q. As a detective, were you required to have a certain standard before you arrested someone?

A. Yes.

Q. What's that standard?

A. Either you witness it or you have a witness that witnessed it.

Q. I take it you didn't witness the murder, correct?

A. No, sir.

Q. Would I be correct then that the basis of the arrest of plaintiff was some type of eyewitness testimony?

A. I specifically don't recall any identification process.

Q. Do you recall at the time that plaintiff was arrested, that his brother was at the precinct charged with murder?

A. No, sir.

Q. You have no independent recollection of that?

A. No, sir.

At this point, the attorney showed the detective a police department document that made reference to a surveillance van and witnesses.

Q. Do you recall as you sit here today ever being in a surveillance van with a confidential informant outside the precinct?

A. I don't recall a confidential informant. I remember an incident where a surveillance vehicle was near the precinct. I don't remember the specifics of why we were there.

Q. Do you ever recall being in a surveillance van in front of the precinct?

A. Yes, sir.

Q. On how many occasions?

A. I could only recall one incident there with a surveillance vehicle.

Q. Having read the document previously marked Exhibit 2, does it refresh your recollection that that was the incident?

A. I'm only assuming that's the incident.

Q. Because you only recall being in the van once?

A. Correct.

Q. Do you recall on that day whether or not a confidential informant was in the van with you?

A. No, sir.

Q. Do you recall whether or not any potential eyewitness was in the van with you?

A. No, sir.

The attorney showed the detective other police department documents and had the detective recount what each document contained.

Q. The next document memorializes your involvement in the surveillance van with a witness, is that correct?

A. Yes, sir.

Q. It says the date and time?

A. Yes.

Q. It says you were present with the above witness in a surveillance van in front of the precinct, did I read that correctly?

A. Yes, sir.

Q. As you sit here today, do you recall why you were with that witness in a surveillance van in front of the precinct?

A. Not specifically, sir, I don't.

Q. Can you think of any reason why you would be with that witness in a surveillance van in front of the precinct?

The witness's counsel directed him not to answer because the question was repetitive and called for speculation.

Q. Can you think of any reasonable explanation why you were with that witness at that time on that date in front of the precinct?

The witness's counsel again directed him not to answer because the question assumed a fact not in evidence.

Then, the examining attorney showed the witness an additional police department document and reviewed it with the witness.

Q. So now we know on the date and time of the arrest, you were in a surveillance van with a witness involved in the murder investigation, sitting in front of the precinct, is that correct?

A. According to the report, yes.

At first, the detective had denied any recollection of the incident, but after the questioning based on the reports, he grudgingly admitted that he had been in a surveillance van outside the police station. By his response to a leading question, he agreed that he was in a surveillance van only once. Then, when he was shown a document that indicated his presence in a surveillance van with a confidential informant, he had to concede the point. Once he conceded that the document correctly recorded his presence in the surveillance van, he could not credibly maintain that the same document incorrectly recorded the presence of the confidential informant.

Although the detective never said outright that he remembered a confidential informant in the van, he essentially agreed to the leading and conclusory question wherein the attorney said, "Now we know … you were in the surveillance van with the witness…." The detective answered, "According to the report, yes."

The detective, evidently, had not thoroughly reviewed the documents. It appeared that he attempted to stonewall, then had to reverse himself. His equivocal and evasive answers could have been the basis for a jury to reasonably infer that he was lying, and when juries believe a police officer is lying, invariably they render liability verdicts against him.

Chapter Five

Survival Tactics for Defendants and Witnesses

What follows is advice for police officers called to testify at depositions. With minor adjustments, it is applicable to all prospective witnesses and defendants in other fields, whether governmental, private enterprise, or personal.

Preparation

When called to a deposition, you should expect and train for a long day. Come to the deposition well rested. Perhaps, do some light exercise before your appearance. Do not wear your police uniform, unless the subpoena so orders. Wear neat, comfortable business attire.

As soon as you are notified, obtain and review pertinent documents and transcripts of prior statements and testimony. Do not wait until shortly before the scheduled date to do this. If the attorney representing you and your agency suggests meeting a day or so before the scheduled date in order to go over the case and review documents, you should insist on doing it immediately. You should give yourself adequate time to absorb the current information, adjust to the circumstances, and revive and reconstruct your memory of the events.

Review the facts as you remember them and prepare a cohesive account of the incident on the basis of your personal observations and knowledge. Note any discrepancies between your present recollection of the incident and the reports and transcripts that you reviewed. Bring any discrepancies to the attention of your attorney, and if you know of explanations, advise your attorney about them.

Conservation

Conserve your energy, which, in this case, means conserve your thinking power. None of us are infallible. When we get tired, we make mental mistakes. So do not let the attorney sap your energy with side issues, irrelevant topics, or minutiae.

Listen to each question and think about each answer. You are not required to give immediate, split-second answers. You do not have to impress anyone with how quickly you can think on your feet, and there is no final examination grade. At the deposition, a judge or jury is not watching you. You may take a few extra seconds to answer without appearing evasive.

Avoid getting into detailed discussions, debates, or long explanations. A good practice is to give simple "yes" or "no" answers, if appropriate. This is usually best during background questions. However, be careful not to be led into an inaccurate "yes" or "no." Some answers may need a qualifier, but you should not volunteer information that is not necessary to answer the question. If the examining attorney wants to explore a subject, let him do the work; let him provide the words. If he does not describe the facts accurately, you can simply say, "no." He will have to rephrase his question properly in order to get you to agree to his description.

Follow a routine pattern: Listen to the question; wait for the questioner to finish; think of the fairest truthful answer; speak as briefly as possible while answering only the question posed; then stop.

Do not suggest or anticipate the next question. If the attorney asks, "Did you discuss the matter in the Wednesday meeting?" If you did not, but discussed the matter at another meeting, do not answer, "Not at that meeting." The attorney may not have known of another meeting and may not have intended to ask a question about it. Make the attorney work for his answers. Simply answer, "No."

During the course of the deposition, if you need a break, take one. You are entitled to take a reasonable number of breaks. Normally, a break cannot be taken when a posed question has not been answered, but if you are physically uncomfortable, you should take a break rather than give an imperfect answer. You may justifiably circumvent the rule by saying, "Please repeat the question" or "I don't understand the question." Then, while the stenographer is retrieving the previous question or before the attorney reformulates his question, ask, "May I take a break now?"

Of course, the number of breaks should be limited, and should not be used as a repeated tactic to avoid legitimate questions.

Perspective

An officer entering a deposition should not expect to win the case by his testimony. His objective should be limited to completing the deposition without compromising his or his agency's side of the case. He must remember that he is part of an adversarial process, and the best approach is to be as truthful as needed, as responsive as possible, and in control. He should neither hide the truth nor unnecessarily volunteer the truth. Moreover, he has to come to terms with the fact that truth and justice may not play any part in deciding the outcome of the case. Venting his emotions at what he may feel is the injustice of the lawsuit or the allegations against him will not help, and will, more likely, cause damage.

Recognition

Understand the tactics the attorney may try to employ, and understand that he may switch from one tactic to another. He may start with tedious questions designed to cause fatigue, then he may switch to high-pressure, rapid-fire questions. Or he may switch from being friendly to being confrontational. When you recognize that he is attempting to employ a particular tactic, do not overreact. Do not acknowledge that you know what he is doing; counteract by employing your own tactics.

When the examining attorney uses a friendly tone to create the impression that the deposition will go easier if the witness is cooperative, remember a friendly attorney is usually a "wolf in sheep's clothing." Don't forget that he is your opponent, and, no matter how well you seem to get along with him, you will not convince him to drop the lawsuit.

Questions asked in a friendly, conversational way have the same weight and importance as questions asked combatively. Listen to the words of the question, not the manner. Think about the proper response, then answer.

If the attorney is combative and argumentative, it is extremely important to avoid trying to match him. Take extra time to answer the questions. Focus on the factual elements of the question. Do not focus on derogatory innuendoes or sarcasm that may be incorporated in the question. Do not let a discourteous demeanor upset you. It is a tactic used by the attorney to rattle witnesses into making mistakes. Counteract by being extra thoughtful, and give your factual answer without showing any signs of an emotional reaction. Your calm demeanor and confidence will most likely persuade him to abandon his combative tactics.

If the attorney tries to pressure you with rapid-fire questions, slow him down by incorporating his question into your answer. The following example illustrates this point:

Q. Officer, what tour of duty were you performing on December 1, 2003?

A. On December 1, 2003, I was performing a four p.m. to midnight tour.

Q. What was your partner's name?

A. My partner's name was Joe Smith.

Q. Was Joe Smith your regular partner?

A. Yes. Joe Smith was my regular partner.

Do Not Be Subservient

Do not call the attorney, "Sir." Do not repeatedly say, "Yes, sir." "That's correct, sir." "You may be right, sir." It sets the wrong tone, and can become extremely tedious after four or five hours. Although you may feel a bit intimidated, or nervous, or uncertain, you should maintain a professional relationship on equal terms.

Maintain Your Options

Do not agree to be locked into answering questions according to the attorney's rules. The attorney will open with a statement, "If you don't understand a question, tell me. Otherwise I'll assume you understand it. Do you agree to that?"

Do not agree. Do not say, "Yes."

Say, "I'll do the best I can," or "I'll try."

Near the end of a segment of the deposition, the attorney may attempt to lock in your answers up to that point. This is often undertaken to trap a witness with prior inconsistent statements or inconsistent documents. The following is an example taken from the deposition of a detective who was being sued for false arrest and negligent investigation:

Q. Have you described to me everything that you did in an investigative capacity concerning this case?

A. To the best of my recollection.

Q. Have you told me everything that you recall specifically discussing with the district attorney's office about this investigation?

A. Yes.

Q. Have you told me everything that you knew about the facts of this investigation?

A. Yes.

You should recognize this as a potential trap. The attorney will not ask these questions unless he has additional information, usually documents, with which to confront you. When an attorney employs this tactic, it is a clear indication that the deposition is not about information gathering; rather, it is about attacking your credibility. Do not lock yourself in. Say, "I don't know. I've told you everything I remember, but there could be something I don't remember."

The attorney will press you to remember everything. Do not submit. Say, "The case was a long time ago. Perhaps, if you have other documents, they might refresh my recollection."

If the attorney takes your suggestion, shows you additional documents, and poses a series of questions, you may respond appropriately. However, at the end of that process, he will ask you again whether you have told him everything. Do not submit. Say, "I don't know. There still could be things I do not recollect." Your rationale for this answer is the truth: people do not remember everything.

At the close of the deposition, the attorney may ask, "Do you want to change any of your answers?"

Do not answer "yes" or "no."

Say, "Without looking at the transcript, I cannot be sure."

After the deposition, a copy of the transcript will be sent to you, which will provide you with the opportunity to make written corrections.

Do Not Volunteer Information

Do not volunteer information that is not called for by the question. This is a cardinal rule that applies even more so to the deposition than to the trial.

At a trial, a skilled attorney will not ask a question to which he does not already know the answer. He will design his questions to get the answer that he wants from the witness and will avoid answers and information that he does not want the judge or jury to hear. If the attorney makes a mistake in his question and leaves an opening, an adversarial witness might be able to answer with the information the attorney was trying to avoid. The witness "volunteers" information but does not violate the cardinal rule because the information is called for by the question.

In contrast to a trial, at a deposition you should not attempt to volunteer additional information even when the question gives you an opening to do so. (An exception to this rule is discussed below).

Answer each question as narrowly as possible and say only what is necessary to provide an honest answer. Remember the attorney may not have all the information, and he may not have realized all the possibilities of what occurred before, during, and after the event. Do not unnecessarily give him information he does not have.

An example of unnecessarily volunteering information occurred in a lawsuit brought on behalf of a plaintiff who had been shot by New York City police officers. The plaintiff was paralyzed as a result of the shooting. Before the shooting, the plaintiff allegedly had brandished an automatic pistol and threatened a bus driver. The police were called and when they approached the plaintiff to question him, the plaintiff first began to walk and then ran away. Several police officers pursued him. The plaintiff allegedly turned and pointed the pistol at the officers, and may have fired one shot at them. The plaintiff continued to flee with the officers in pursuit. The officers testified that at several points the plaintiff turned and pointed the pistol at them. He appeared to be racking the gun, which is a maneuver to clear a jammed bullet. During the pursuit, five officers fired a total of forty-seven shots. The majority of the bullets missed, until the end of the pursuit when the plaintiff was shot and apprehended.

The pistol was recovered from the plaintiff with an unspent bullet in the chamber that had a firing pin mark on the primer. Other unspent bullets, including one expended bullet shell casing from the plaintiff's gun, were recovered along the pursuit path. The physical evidence indicated that the plaintiff apparently had fired one shot, attempted to shoot again, but the pistol had jammed and he discarded the jammed bullets.

The plaintiff had a criminal record for violent crimes, and at the time of the incident a warrant had been issued for his arrest on another gun possession charge. Nevertheless, after a ballistics examination found that the plaintiff's pistol was inoperable, a decision was made by the district attorney's office to dismiss the criminal charges against the plaintiff. The fact that the plaintiff was paralyzed was likely an important factor in the decision to dismiss the criminal charges.

After the dismissal, plaintiff's attorney brought a civil suit against the police alleging they had acted negligently, recklessly, and violated the plaintiff's civil rights.

During the discovery phase of the civil suit, the plaintiff was deposed and testified that his friend had placed the gun in his belt. He admitted that he ran from the police and held the gun in his hand because he did not want it to fall out of his pants. He denied shooting at the officers.

The five police officers gave depositions, and their narratives were essentially consistent. All testified that they observed the plaintiff at various times point his gun at them, although only two could testify that they actually saw the plaintiff fire his weapon.

One of the officers at his deposition volunteered information to the examining attorney beyond the what was called for by the question.

The attorney questioned the officer regarding a point during the chase when the plaintiff stopped and turned with his weapon. The attorney asked the officer:

Q. Do you know if the gun actually fired at that point?

A. There were a lot of bangs going on. There were other people shooting as well as myself. I couldn't differentiate his gun shooting to someone else's shooting.

What's wrong with this answer? Although it is truthful, it is a prime example of volunteering information unnecessarily.

It seems the officer did not know whether the gun actually fired at the point. He should have answered, simply, "No" or "I don't know" or "I don't recall."

Instead, he volunteered information that provided the attorney with a theory of contagious shooting. Contagious shooting occurs when a second police officer sees or hears a first officer firing at a suspect, and the second officer assumes the suspect must have pointed or fired at the first officer. The second officer then fires at the suspect, although he did not actually see the suspect point or fire his weapon. When other officers see or hear the first and second officers firing, they join in and assist by firing their weapons.

The attorney, after obtaining this volunteered evidence, was able to gear his questions to the other officers in order to elicit corroborating evidence from them about the possibility of contagious shooting.

Do Not Volunteer an Emotional Response

Another example of volunteering information that was not called for by the question occurred in a case in which a Philadelphia police officer reacted emotionally to the deposition process. It is not uncommon for witnesses, including police officers, to become emotional during testimony, and the length and intensity of deposition testimony increases the chances of emotionalism. The deposition process has similarities to police interrogations, and both processes sometimes induce subjects to make admissions or even confessions.

In the Philadelphia case, the officer had arrested a plaintiff for interfering with an arrest and for resisting arrest. At one point, the officer had used force that caused the plaintiff's forehead to hit a doorframe at the police station. During the deposition, the attorney questioned the officer about what was said between the officer and the plaintiff before the arrest.

Q. Did he say anything further at that point in time?

A. Well, the thing that upsets me—I'm a little upset, ma'am.

At this point the officer's counsel interrupted: "Don't talk about what upsets you, just give her an answer to the question."

The officer's counsel called for a break. It didn't help. When the questioning resumed, the examining attorney already had the opening she needed.

Q. What did he say?

A. He kept repeating … about me bothering the trespasser, and he made references to "You wouldn't do that to me?"

Q. Why was that statement upsetting to you?

A. The statement was not upsetting to me, the situation was upsetting to me.

Q. What about the situation was upsetting to you?

A. Plaintiff placed me in a precarious situation where if the trespasser became violent, I could have gotten hurt.

The officer did not answer yes or no, but volunteered his state of mind, and gave the plaintiff attorney the ammunition that he was "upset." No doubt, she would use that ammunition before the jury.

Later, during the same deposition, this officer volunteered more information.

After the arrest, the officer had taken the plaintiff to a hospital to get stitches. The attorney asked him about conversations that took place there.

Q. While you were at the hospital, did you have any discussion with plaintiff about a deal?

A. I said, 'No, you're going to Central Booking.' I explained to him that he is a keeper.

Q. You told him that he was a 'keeper'?

A. A keeper. The only thing that I said to him was, "If you didn't escalate everything as much as you did, you probably would have just gotten a summons."

The attorney did not pursue these answers here, but no doubt at trial in front of a jury she would make the officer explain that a "keeper" was a term adapted from fishing jargon. A fish that is large enough to keep rather than thrown back is a "keeper." In police parlance, a person who could be arrested, put in jail overnight, and taken to court, rather than issued a summons and released, is a "keeper." Comparing a person to a fish is demeaning and would certainly be exploited by the attorney.

Do Not Be Persuaded to Keep Talking

There may be times when an attorney will attempt to induce the witness to provide more expansive answers. He may do this directly by asking the witness to try to recall other information or facts, or he may imply that the answer is incomplete or untruthful. He may express by his demeanor or tone of voice that he is not happy with the answer and ask, "Is that all?" Or, "Is that your final answer?" He may repeat the question, speaking slowly or with more emphasis. If your first answer was truthful and responsive, do not change it.

A witness should not feel compelled to expand upon his answer merely to please the attorney. He can answer, "That's all I currently remember."

Sometimes, after an answer, an attorney will remain silent. Many people feel that silence is a vacuum that needs to be filled. We have all experienced the discomfort of an awkward break in a conversation, and we try to think of something to say to allay the discomfort. During a deposition, saying something to break the silence must be avoided. Remain silent, and wait for the next question. In such a situation, silence is golden.

I Don't Know versus I Don't Recall

When questioned about past events, if you do not know the answer because you were not present or did not observe the event or part of the event, say, "I don't know." To show that you are cooperative and truthful, you can explain your position with qualifiers, such as, "Someone told me that afterward, but I didn't see it for myself." Or, "I read that in a report, but I don't have any firsthand knowledge of that."

If you were present and may have observed the event but cannot remember, say, "I don't recall" or "I don't remember." If you genuinely do not remember, stick to that answer. Many attorneys will attempt to press you to change it. A simple example occurs when an attorney asked an officer whether the siren and turret lights of his patrol car were on when the officer responded to a routine accident scene.

Q. When you drove to the scene did you employ your siren?

A. I don't remember.

Q. Were the turret lights of your vehicle on?

A. I don't remember.

Q. Would it have been normal procedure to have them on when responding to an accident?

A. Depends.

Q. But there would have been nothing unusual about having them on, would there be?

A. No.

Q. Have you utilized lights and sirens to respond to other accident cases?

A. Yes.

Q. It was dark when this accident occurred. Correct?

A. Yes.

Q. You responded to this accident as quickly as you could?

A. Yes.

Q. When you respond to an accident, do you try to do so as safely as possible?

A. Yes.

Q. In this case, do you remember not responding as safely as possible?

A. No.

Q. So, as far as you remember, you responded as quickly and as safely as possible. Is that correct?

A. I think so.

Q. Lights and siren would both help you respond quickly and safely. True?

A. True.

Q. So it's possible or probable that you used your lights and siren?

A. It's possible.

Q. You generally consider yourself an officer who tries to do things in the safest manner possible?

A. Sure.

Q. So, responding to an accident when it was dark out, and responding quickly and safely as possible, you probably used either your turret lights or your siren?

A. Probably.

Q. You might have used both.

A. Probably.

Assuming the officer did not remember using his turret lights or siren, he should not have conceded that he "probably" did. Factual testimony should not be based on probabilities.

However, an officer must avoid getting trapped into a non-credible litany of "I don't recall" or "I don't recollect." As a sworn witness you have an obligation to answer the questions to the best of your ability. If it appears that you are using "I don't recall" simply to avoid answering the questions, at the trial the attorney will be able to portray you as uncooperative and as someone purposefully hiding something.

An extraordinary example of a witness who attempted to avoid answering questions by relying on "I do not recollect" occurred in the case of *Perlman Rim Corporation v. Firestone Tire and Rubber Company*. The plaintiff, Perlman, filed a patent infringement suit against Firestone. When he took the witness stand, the cross-examining attorney attempted to impeach his credibility by asking him whether twenty years earlier he had been arrested in England, had jumped bail and was a fugitive from justice. Perlman denied remembering any such incident. Near the end of the long cross-examination, the judge lost patience with Perlman and took over the examination.

Court:

Q. "You have no recollection of any part of what he has told you?"

Perlman:

A. "I have not."

Q. "And you will not deny it in whole or in part? I do not understand that?"

A. "I cannot deny what I do not remember to have happened."

Q. "So that I understand, in respect of all this testimony, that it may have happened to you but you do not recollect it, is that it?"

A. "I have no recollection of any such thing as that."

Q. "Please answer my question. It may have happened to you but you do not recall it. Can you not recall it?"

A. "I cannot admit that it happened to me because I do not remember it."

Q. "I do not ask you whether you admit it. I said, your position is that it may have happened to you but you do not recall it, is that your position?"

A. "No, sir."

Q. "It is not your position?"

A. "It is not my position."

Q. "Your position is, then, that it did not happen, it could not have happened?"

A. "I have no recollection of any such incident as that happening."

Q. "You keep taking refuge in that, which as you know perfectly well by now is not what I want you to answer, and is not what I mean by my question. I press you again, is it your position that this may have happened to you but you do not recall it?"

A. "Had it happened I would have recalled it."

Q. "If it had happened you would have recalled it?"

A. "I would have remembered it."

Q. "So therefore you deny that it happened, do you?"

A. "I cannot state that it happened, because I have no recollection of it."

Q. "Very good, you say it could not have happened to you?"

A. "It could not have happened without my remembering it."

Q. "It could not have happened without your remembering it, is that your position?"

A. "It would not appear so to me."

Q. "I do not know what would appear to you. I want you to think now, as you are on your oath, whether it could have happened to you and you have forgotten it; because I shall take that as an equivalent to a denial, which it certainly is. Now I ask you, is it your position that that could not have happened to you, and therefore did not happen to you?"

A. "Well, your Honor, I have no recollection of any such occurrence as that."

Q. "Now, if you continue to trifle with me I shall have to take some action on it. I shall have to commit you until you answer the question as I put it to you. I will give you plenty of opportunity. I say, is it your position that the things, the arrest and the general circumstances, could not and did not happen to you?"

A. "I cannot say that they did not happen."

Q. "They might have happened to you and you have forgotten it? Take your time."

A. "If they happened, I do not remember them."

Q. "Might they have happened and you have forgotten them? I will give you two more chances, and if you do not answer I shall commit you."

A. "Possibly it may have happened and I do not remember them."

Q. "Is it your position that you might have been arrested in England, under the circumstances detailed to you, and you have forgotten it, forgotten all about it?"

A. "It may be."[1]

Do Not Debate

Witnesses have attempted to debate a point or match wits with attorneys. For police officers, such an attempt should be saved for the debating society. During a deposition it serves no purpose.

---

1. Francis Wellman, The Art of Cross-Examination (New York: MacMillan, 1936), 135-36.

Reprinted with the permission of Scribner, an imprint of Simon & Schuster Adult Publishing Group, from *The Art of Cross-Examination* by Francis Wellman. Copyright 1936 by the Macmillan Company, copyright renewed 1964 by Ethel Wellman.

In this case alleging police brutality, the attorney was attempting to determine the distance between an officer and his partner when the plaintiff, Miss Smith, jumped on the partner's back.

Q. When you made these observations, how far were you from Miss Smith?

A. I didn't measure the distance.

Q. I'm not asking you for an exact measurement, my question to you was if you can tell us the approximate distance between yourself and Miss Smith when you made these observations.

A. I can't give you an approximate distance.

Q. Sir, were you as close to her as you are to me right now?

A. No.

Q. Were you farther away?

A. Yes.

Q. Were you as far away as the door, which is to your left?

A. I believe it was a little bit farther away than that.

Q. Sir, do you know distances in terms of feet? You know what a foot is?

A. Yes.

Q. Was it more than ten feet?

A. I didn't measure it.

Q. Sir, I'm not asking for an exact measurement but for an approximation.

A. Didn't enter my mind to approximate that distance when I observed that.

Q. I'm sure it didn't enter your mind. I'm talking now that it occurred, can you tell me what you approximate the distance was at the time that you made this observation?

A. I can't approximate it.

Q. Is that because you cannot recall or because you don't know how to measure the distance?

A. It's because of the amount of time involved.

Q. So your memory fails you to some degree and you cannot recall; is that correct?

A. Didn't say my memory is failing me. It's been a long time since I've been there and a long time since the observation.

Q. What about the length of time prevents you from estimating the distance?

A. Because I never committed that to memory to begin with.

Q. So you have no memory of it; is that correct?

A. I didn't say that.

Q. I'm asking you if that is correct.

A. That's not correct.

Q. So when you say you never committed it to memory, what do you mean by that, sir?

A. Again, I'll state now as I stated before, when I made that observation, when I first saw Miss Smith, the distance she was away from me was not a concern.

Q. That was not my question. My question to you, sir, is: What about the passage of time prevents you from telling us what the distance was approximately from Miss Smith at the time you made these observations?

A. I thought I already answered that.

Q. Well, then I apologize for having you answer it again. Would you answer it, please?

A. It's not so much passage of time, it's just a general recollection of a very vague or general distance.

Q. What is your general recollection of that general or vague distance?

A. You already bracketed it, further away than the door.

Q. Sir, when you say "further away than the door," would you agree with me that that would be approximately ten feet?

A. No.

Q. You wouldn't?

A. Unless you have a tape ruler.

Q. Sir, I do have a tape ruler. Would you like us to measure that?

A. That's up to you.

Q. Let's use my foot. That's about twelve inches, right. I will measure from the door to you and we'll count. You tell me how many feet that is.

At this point, the attorney measured by stepping one foot at a time to the door.

Q. Can we agree that's about ten feet?

A. It's short of ten feet. It's ten of your feet.

Q. We'll use that as the measurement of my feet.

A. Short of ten feet.

Q. Short of ten of my feet.

A. Yes.

So the officer finally agreed that the distance in question was short of ten feet. Was the fight worth it? Since the officer had already testified that he saw the confrontation, and testified with some specificity, it served little purpose to refuse to given an approximate distance. It would have saved much of the officer's mental energy to have answered the first question with a broad approximation, and would have avoided the impression that the officer was an uncooperative, recalcitrant witness.

Do Not Endeavor to Remember Every Detail

People are not expected to remember every detail of their lives. Witnesses should not attempt to exaggerate their powers of recall because a common sense jury is likely to infer that their testimony is contrived. In a 1991 case, a police officer was sued for a shooting that occurred while the officer was off-duty and drinking in a bar. The theory of the plaintiff's case was that the officer was drunk and he unnecessarily shot and killed the plaintiff. During the officer's deposition, which was taken six years after the shooting, the following testimony was taken:

Q. Did you have anything else to drink in the bar that night?

A. Yes, from the first beer I ordered, as I was talking to several

patrons, the bartender, I guess, picked up my beer, which was maybe half full and he disposed of it thinking it was somebody's throw away beer and when I turned and finally - I would say, I really can't say how long after I was socializing but it had to be a good twenty minutes and I turned and the beer was gone. I mentioned to the bartender 'I had my beer on the bar' and he was like 'Oh, I might have picked it up by accident and threw it away,' so, he replaced it with a full one.

Q. Was this on the house?

A. On the house.

Q. And did you consume that beer?

A. I had a couple of sips of that beer and was holding it in my hand at that time because I didn't want him to throw it away by mistake again because it was pretty busy in the bar.

The officer's unnecessarily detailed memory of the drinks he had exhibited either a contrived account or an unusual attachment to beer. Neither conclusion helped the officer's case.

Do Not Agree to Absolutes

You may be asked whether you always follow certain rules, procedures, or practices or whether you ever violate certain rules, procedures, or practices. Do not say you "always" followed the rules exactly. Do not say you "never" violated any rules. If the attorney asks about them, you can be sure he is doing so because he has a contradictory instance up his sleeve.

Instead say something to the effect, "I have always tried to follow certain rules or practices, unless I had a particular reason not to, or unless I made a mistake without knowing it."

Getting out the Primary, Necessary, and Important Fact

An exception to the "do not volunteer information" rule applies to the crucial information that a defendant must get on the record or risk loss of the case by omission. This testimony should be vetted with the defendant's counsel beforehand, kept to a minimum, and limited to the core facts necessary for the defendant.

In cases of a police shooting, in which the officer fired because he was threatened with a gun or other weapon, he must be sure to get on the record the facts that made him feel his life was in danger.

If an officer had been off-duty at the time of an incident, he may need to establish that his actions were within the scope of his employment as a police officer as opposed to actions in his individual capacity for personal reasons. Basic facts, such as displaying his badge, identifying himself as a police officer, and attempting to make an arrest in connection with a crime, or in an emergency situation to protect life and property, must be part of his testimony.

In a false arrest and excessive force case resulting from an incident that occurred in 1997, the arresting officer was deposed in 2000. The officer had arrested a woman for driving while intoxicated. She allegedly resisted arrest. The officer used force to subdue her, and her arm was broken. During the deposition, the plaintiff's attorney questioned the officer about what led up to the arrest. His goal was to show that the officer did not have probable cause to make the arrest, and, therefore, the subsequent use of force that resulted in the broken arm was unlawful. His questioning pursued the following line:

Q. What is happening next now?

A. I was making observations of her clothing and her speech and the manner, gait.

Q. What do you recall about her clothing?

A. She looked disheveled.

Q. Please tell me what you meant by that.

A. Her clothes looked like she had slept in them.

Q. Anything else?

A. Her footwear; one was a pink slipper, and the other looked like a shoe.

Q. Did you ask her about that, why she was wearing two different shoes?

A. Not then. Later.

Q. Do you recall anything she subsequently told you why she had a slipper on that day?

A. There was talk of a prior foot injury or broken toe.

Q. You said you made some observations about speech. Can you tell me what you recall about that?

A. A very thick slurred speech.

Q. And you said you made some observations about gait. What can you tell me about that?

A. When she was leaning on her car, she had slid to the left and stopped and she had slid to the right sometimes.

Q. Did you inquire as to whether or not she was on any medications?

A. I asked her if she had been drinking.

Q. What was her response?

A. She said no.

Q. Did you inquire whether or not she was on any medications?

A. I don't think so.

Q. Did you make any other observations about her other than what you told us about the gait, the speech, and the clothing?

At this point, apparently the officer's counsel sensed that the officer was going to answer in the negative, so he called for a break. This was not appropriate, as a break should not be taken while a question is pending. He got away with it. The plaintiff's attorney did not object and consented to the break.

The question pending was extremely important because the officer arguably had not provided sufficient facts to substantiate the probable cause necessary for an arrest. Disheveled clothes and even slurred speech do not establish intoxication. The plaintiff's pink slipper was explained by her broken toe, which also could explain her unsteady gait. The officer needed to "volunteer" more information, and on the break, his counsel may have emphasized that point to him.

The questioning resumed.

Q. I was asking you if you made any other observations about her other than what you already told us?

A. Yes. The nature of the accident itself. That she sideswiped a parked trailer. She was unsteady on her feet. She was loud. She was abusive, slurred speech. She looked disheveled, two different slippers on. She mentioned scotch twice.

The additional points noted by the officer helped establish probable cause. Had the officer not added them, his defense would have been greatly weakened.

Leaving crucial facts out of deposition testimony can have adverse legal ramifications, and can be used against an officer at trial. Deposition testimony of a party may be read to the jury at trial. If the police officer does not get the favorable information on the deposition record, subsequently at trial, when he testifies to the favorable information, the plaintiff's attorney may point out that the officer did not mention this information at the deposition. The attorney may argue that the officer recently fabricated the information to protect himself and his department, and may embellish this argument by characterizing any conversations the officer had with other officers or his attorney as a conspiracy in connection with the "new" testimony.

Therefore, it is imperative that your deposition testimony includes information essential to your position. If there were no opportunity to do so during the questioning, at the end of the deposition, make a short statement.

Or, ask for a break, then confer with your attorney to have him ask you the pertinent questions to elicit the necessary information.

Realize you not only need to defend your agency and the role you played as an employee of the agency, but you need to defend yourself against potential personal liability. If the jury finds you liable for your actions and they award punitive damages against you, your employer may not indemnify you for that judgment. The purpose of punitive damages is to punish; therefore, the law discourages your employer from paying the damages on your behalf. You will have to pay and your personal assets may be seized.

Exact Measurements of Distance and Time

Stick to approximations. Unless you took measurements or recorded the time, do not give a precise measurement or an exact time. Give a bracketed approximation. Say, "I don't know exactly, but it was approximately between thirty and forty feet." Or, "Between ten and thirty seconds."

Once you have given your best recollection, do not be manipulated into a more precise answer.

In the following testimony, the examining attorney maneuvered an officer into testifying to a distance of which the officer was uncertain.

Q. How far away from you was the plaintiff you first saw him?

A. Approximately 30 to 40 feet.

Q. Could it have been more than 40 feet?

A. Possibly. I'm not exactly sure.

Q. More than 41 feet?

A. Maybe.

Q. More than 42 feet?

A. It could have been.

Q. So when you said 'approximately 30 to 40 feet,' you weren't sure it was within that distance?

A. That's correct.

Q. So it's possible that the distance was more than 42 feet.

A. It's possible.

The question of distance may have been an important element of the plaintiff's case, and the officer gave the attorney either ammunition to attack the reliability of his testimony or a fact that the attorney could use in his summation

Since the officer did not know the exact distance and was only providing an estimate, he should have stuck with his initial answer. When asked if it could have been forty-one feet, he should have said, "I think it was approximately between thirty and forty feet."

Estimations of how much time elapsed during a traumatic incident are extremely unreliable. Nevertheless, attorneys will attempt to pin a witness down to a specific time because they need to establish a time line for their presentation during the trial. The following is an example:

Q. After you lost sight of the male Hispanic, how much time passes before you again regain sight of him and you see Officer Blank getting off of him?

A. I have no idea.

Q. Let us see if you can estimate it. It is less than an hour; right?

A. You're killing me. Yes, it's less than an hour.

Q. Is it less than five minutes?

A. Are you trying to pinpoint me to a time?

Q. I am not trying to pinpoint you. I am not trying to trick you.

A. I am trying to be helpful here. I just don't know the time or the time frame. I am all pumped up. At this point in time, I could say six hours.

Q. I understand you were not standing there looking at your watch, but you also have knowledge of the incident and I am trying to get knowledge of the incident.

A. I understand. To the best of my recollection, I would say it's like two minutes, you know, something like that.

Witness' Counsel: That is just a guess?

A. Of course.

Q. I do not want you to guess. I want you to give me your best estimate.

Witness' Counsel: The witness said a number of times he does not know.

Q. I do not want you to speculate and I do not want you to guess. I want you to give me your best estimate of how much time elapsed between the time you last saw this male Hispanic.

Witness' Counsel: Stop badgering him.

Plaintiff's Attorney: I am not badgering him. I resent the implication. I am trying to conduct the deposition.

Witness' Counsel: I understand what you are trying to do.

Q. Is that your final answer, two minutes?

A. If you want to go with that, fine. That's my best.

Q. During this time frame of approximately two minutes, what, if anything, are you doing?

Witness' Counsel: Note my objection. You can answer.

Q. You lost sight of him and approximately two minutes later you see Officer Blank get off this male Hispanic. During the approximately two minutes, what are you doing?

A. I am still holding my position, waiting for the guy to walk toward me.

The time line was extremely important because the case involved a fast-moving incident during which six police officers fired their guns at two men who were intoxicated and armed with knives. The two men were brothers, and both were killed. Their families sued the police department. During the depositions, the accounts given by the six officers naturally varied from one to another, and the plaintiff attorney sought to emphasize any discrepancies that would make a case of wrongful action by the police.

In the event that an officer cannot be specific with respect to elapsed time, he should provide a broad approximation only. In the above case, something on the order of one to four minutes would have been acceptable.

Switching of Topics and Interruptions

At a deposition, examining attorneys frequently avoid or circumvent questions that would elicit answers favorable to the police position. Instead, they pose questions that emphasize what the police did wrong, but avoid questions that allow the police witness to explain why their actions were correct and reasonable under the circumstances. To tire or confuse a witness, attorneys will switch from subject to subject or mix up the chronology of the incident in question. During testimony when the witness is attempting to describe the events from his or her point of view, attorneys often interrupt the answer and switch to another subject. When this occurs, the officer may fail to impart necessary information favorable to the police position.

Therefore, during a deposition, when giving the essential part of your statement, do not allow yourself to be cut off or have the subject switched. Know that you are allowed to finish your answers. Even when you have completed your answer, and the attorney has asked a new question, you can revisit the previous question by saying for example, "Excuse me, regarding that prior answer, I want to add that…."

In the case in which six officers shot and killed the two knife-wielding brothers, one of the officers tried to complete his account of the incident from his perspective, but the attorney attempted to interrupt him. The officer persisted and succeeded in giving a full account of the incident. Perhaps, he volunteered too much information, and, perhaps, he should have saved most of his account for the trial. However, depositions often become cathartic events for police officers who have had to shoot and kill a human being. When given the opportunity to explain what happened to them, they tell all, as evidenced by the following example:

Q. What else did you do after that?

A. I pointed my gun at him, and I began a long series of asking him to stop. I started screaming, "Stop. Drop the knife. Stop. Drop the knife." And it just came recycled and recycled to the point where I'm pleading with him to drop the knife. He turns to run with the knife still in his hand. At this point there's a collection of police officers surrounding him, blocking his path. He ran back and forth. Everyone is screaming at him, "Stop. Drop the knife." And

it goes on what feels like forever. And I'm saying, I've never seen this. In ten years as a police officer, I've never seen somebody attack the police. He was running frantically between the two collections of police officers with uniforms and guns and at no point became rational enough to drop that knife. He was frantic, frantic.

Q. Let me stop you there. The officers that were on the scene at this point, they came from the crime scene nearby?

A. Some of them.

Q. Do you know where the others came from?

A. Some had been brought in to help establish the crime scene up the block.

Q. And the ten or so officers that are on the scene, are they all in uniform?

A. The majority.

Q. When you saw this man running back and forth what, if anything, was he saying?

A. Nothing. He never said a word.

Q. Can you describe what he is doing?

A. I remember saying to myself, This is bad. He's going to -

Q. Hold it a second.

Witness' Counsel: He was not finished.

Plaintiff's Attorney: He was not answering my question.

Witness' Counsel: Maybe he was getting to the answer.

Q. My question was: What was he doing? Not what you are thinking.

A. He's running frantically back and forth with a twelve-inch steak knife in his hand.

Q. You said to him, stop and drop the knife, right?

A. I said, "Stop. Stop. Drop the knife. Drop the knife."

Q. Do you recall approximately how many times you said this? I would not expect you to keep count, of course, but was it once, was it ten times, was it something in the middle there?

A. It was over fifty times.

Q. How close did he get to any of the officers?

A. Five feet, seven feet.

Q. What happened next?

A. Then he started to scrunch down. And he went down into a catcher's position. The knife trailed the floor between his legs, with the tip of the knife just about touching the pavement.

Q. How far away from you right now was he during this time he was kneeling, crouching down?

A. Within three to five feet.

Q. Are you still shielded by the car at this point?

A. No.

Q. What's between you?

A. Nothing.

Q. So at some point you moved from behind the car?

A. I didn't move from behind the car. He came around the car at me.

Q. Let me back you up a second ... At what point did he leave the side-walk and enter the street.

A. He could not go anywhere, so he bolted out into the street and around the car. I went from being one of the few offices that were safe to being pinned against a car. I had nowhere - the only thing I could have done, was turn my back to him with his knife and hope that I could run faster than he could run and stab. So I didn't run. I wanted to run, but I couldn't run. My feet wouldn't move. And I remember thinking, you know, don't this beat all. This is, like, my problem now.

Q. The car, he walked around the back of the car, the rear of the car.

Witness' Counsel: Note my objection to the form of the question.

A. He went around the rear of the car.

Q. What kind of car was it, do you know?

A. It was a big car.

Witness' Counsel: Are you all right? Do you want to take a break?

A. I'm all right. I'm good.

Q. Can you describe for me what, if anything, happened next?

A. He started to rise, to stand. It wasn't a jump up. It was a slow creep.

Q. Was it gradual?

A. Very gradual. I remember him getting bigger and bigger, and he's looking at me as he's rising.... At the point in which he is almost fully erect, the screams, "Drop the knife" become very loud, and it sort of hits me that he's standing ... I'm looking at his eyes, and I see the knife rise ... The knife comes up to about a shoulder length ... he came in a stepping motion, you know, in a lunge.

Q. Did he complete one step or more than one step towards you?

A. No, he did not.

Q. What, if anything, happened next?

A. I fired.

Q. How many rounds did you fire?

A. I'm told a total of ten rounds were fired from my gun.

Q. Do you have an independent recollection?

A. I remember distinctly the first one.

Shortly before this case was scheduled for trial, the City of New York settled the case to avoid the risk of a possible jury verdict in favor of the grieved families of the deceased brothers.

Challenges to Truthfulness

A challenge to a person's truthfulness can be extremely disconcerting. Do not fall into the trap of getting angry.

If asked, "Officer, do you really expect us to believe that?"

Don't say, "I don't care what you believe." Don't retaliate.

Say, "I gave you my answer."

If the attorney persists, say, "Is that a question about the incident?"

If the attorney asks, "Officer, how do you explain the contradictory answer you gave before and the answer you gave now?"

Don't say, "I don't recall." Or, "I can't explain."

Say, "I answered in response to how I understood your line of questions."

He may ask you to explain the difference in your understanding of his earlier questions and the current line of questions.

Do not attempt to reconstruct the prior questions and answers. Say, "I don't remember all your questions. If you want to ask me about the facts of the situation, I'll answer to the best of my ability."

Do Not Lie

Officers occasionally have shown a tendency to evade or tell half-truths regarding what they consider irrelevant or minor matters. Some officers, though generally truthful, have made the mistake of lying. This can have devastating consequences. Most cases come down to a question of credibility, i.e., which side the jury believes. If an officer is caught in one lie, even for a small matter, it may destroy his entire testimony. Juries make allowances for plaintiffs and civilian witness but not for police officers.

Occasionally, an officer on the witness stand will not tell the truth about an immaterial matter, such as not being on his proper post or being engaged in some infraction of his duties at the time of the incident. It is far better to admit the infraction than to attempt to cover it up and be caught in a lie.

Never say such things as, "To be perfectly honest with you, I'm ..." Or, "I'm not going to lie to you ..." It is a given that a witness should give truthful answers only. There is no need to imply you have any reason to lie about the incident.

Be Honest about Profanity

Although inadvisable, it is not uncommon for officers to use profanity or other abusive language in connection with the use of physical force. When questioned about using profanity or abusive language, an officer may be reluctant to admit having used such language. He must be cognizant, however, that the examining attorney has already interviewed other witnesses and knows what they will say. If the other witnesses have stated that the officer used profanity, the attorney will make it part of his game plan to get the officer to deny using profanity. The attorney wants to induce the officer to lie. Catching an officer in a lie by presenting contradictory evidence before a jury is a triumphant moment for an attorney.

The following is an example of locking-in an officer's denial.

Q. After you shot the plaintiff and he was on the ground, what did you say to him?

A. I don't recall.

Q. Did you curse at him?

A. No.

Q. Did you call him any derogatory names.

A. No.

Q. Use any ethnic slurs?

A. No.

Q. Any racial slurs?

A. No.

Q. Did you say, 'Stop, you fuckin' nigger'?

A. No. I did not.

Q. Did you hear any other officers use profanity?

A. No.

Q. Did you hear any other officers use racial slurs?

A. No.

In the above case, the attorney was pleased with the answers because he was hoping that the plaintiff's neighbors, one of whom was a reverend, would testify at trial that they heard officers cursing and using racial epithets. In that event, whom would the jury believe: the officer or the neighbors and the reverend?

The officer in this case handled the questioning well and was not contradicted. Had he used profanity, a simple, "Yes," would be the best answer. Admitting the use of profanity is not as damaging as being caught in a lie about it.

Under some circumstances profanity can be explained. An officer may have used profanity or rough language to let a suspect know the officer meant business or to warn the suspect that the officer might shoot.

If an officer is not sure of the exact words he used, he should not be induced into agreeing to the words suggested by the attorney. He should be aware that attorneys often fish for information. The attorney may or may not have witnesses to the officer's cursing or racial epithets. There might be witnesses who had heard cursing but are now unsure of the exact words or who had cursed.

The officer, depending on what he remembers, should say, "I know I used profanity, but I'm not sure of the exact words I used," or "I may have used profanity, but I don't have a clear recollection."

Should the attorney persists in his attempt to pin down the officer to exact words and even suggest the words used, the officer should not concede to them unless he remembers the exact words he uttered and should stick to "I'm not sure of the exact words." If he admits to exact words, those words will become evidence, even though the attorney may not have had independent proof of them and was merely guessing at them.

Do Not Lie about Racial Slurs

The use of racial slurs, especially by a white officer against a member of a minority group, is a critical hot-button issue. Racial slurs can turn the justifiable use of force into unjustifiable force. Racial slurs can turn an impartial police investigation into a police conspiracy to frame a member of a minority group.

Questions about racial slurs are not limited to their use during the time of the incident in issue. If racial prejudice was a possible motive or influencing factor in the police conduct, the attorney may ask about the use of racial slurs or other demonstrations of prejudice that occurred before or after the time of the incident. Remember Detective Mark Fuhrman with the "N-word" in the O.J. Simpson criminal case.

Questions about the "N-word" or other racial slurs may be relevant if there are grounds to believe that racial animus is an issue. In the Simpson case, the judge allowed the attorney, F. Lee Bailey, to ask Fuhrman whether he had ever used the word. Some would argue that it was not relevant and the judge should not have allowed that line of questioning. However, the judge did allow such questioning, and Fuhrman denied ever using the word.

The denial gave Bailey the opportunity to present collateral evidence to disprove Fuhrman's denial. He brought in a witness who testified she had been working on a screenplay with Fuhrman years before the murders and had tapes of him using the racial epithet in question numerous times. This evidence was admissible because it contracted Fuhrman's denial and had a bearing on his credibility, which is always relevant. More important, it portrayed Fuhrman as a racist and indirectly tainted his entire testimony. It raised the possibility of racial animus as the motivation for a police conspiracy to frame Simpson.

If Fuhrman had answered, "Yes," he, indeed, had used the word, it most likely would have been the end of issue. Under normal legal standards, there would have been no grounds for Bailey to bring in collateral evidence to contradict Fuhrman.

During depositions, attorneys often ask police officers similar questions, and because the relevancy standards in depositions are so lenient, the attorney can explore the issue even when the officer admits using racial slurs.

In a 1990 lawsuit, a question arose about whether racial slurs were transmitted over the police radio. At the deposition, the attorney questioned an officer in the following manner:

Q. These radio-transmissions, you've listened to them since the night of the occurrence, haven't you?

A. Yes.

Q. Have you, sir, ever in your lifetime used the word nigger?

A. Yes, I have.

Q. More than once?

A. No. When I was in Narcotics, I was debriefing an informant who was using the word nigger quite a bit, and I told him to knock the nigger word off.

Q. Other than that, have you ever used the work nigger in your life?

A. No. No. I had a roommate and we were listening to rap music. I was singing the words that were in the lyrics. One of the words was nigger.

Q. But it was just you parroting the words, not you using your own words?

A. I never directed that word in a derogatory sense at any person of African-American descent; I never used that word towards anyone in a derogatory fashion.

Q. Have you ever used it in a joke?

A. No.

Q. You told us all of the occasions in which you used the word nigger, is that accurate?

A. Yes, that's accurate.

The officer in this case, although he apparently tried to be forthcoming, placed himself in a vulnerable position. He denied using the word at any time other than the two instances he mentioned. If the attorney had witnesses or other evidence to contradict the officer, especially if he had evidence that the officer used racial slurs in a disparaging manner, the officer's credibility would be undermined, as Fuhrman's credibility had been in the Simpson case.

The officer should not have agreed that those were the only times he used the word. He should have said, "There may have been other times, but I cannot recall any at the moment."

Have You Discussed the Case?

Unless absolutely true, the officer should neither fall into the trap of saying he never discussed the facts of the case with anyone nor give unconvincing answers about what was said.

It is not likely that the officer will remember exactly what was said, but if he is forthright, he can avoid the implications of a cover-up. He might start by saying, "To the best of my recollection, and I'm sure these are not the exact words." Then, if he can honestly do so, he should try to recount some brief parts of the conversations. If the conversations were self-serving, it can work to the officer's advantage. What better way to get information out that explains the circumstances from the officer's perspective?

Impeachment by Prior Inconsistent Statements

Police officers are often confronted with prior inconsistent statements that they made at a criminal court hearing or a trial or an internal departmental investigation.

If, at a deposition, you are confronted with an inconsistent statement, but the discrepancy is of a relatively minor nature, do not overreact. For instance, differences between 20 and 30 feet are understandable. Simply admit the discrepancy.

If the differences are substantial and material to the case, you will be subjected to intense cross-examination and, barring a reasonable and believable explanation, you will have difficulty maintaining your credibility. That is why it is imperative that you review all of your previous statements and reports before the deposition. If you find discrepancies during your review, you should bring them to the attention of your counsel.

Confronted with Errors or Omissions in Reports

When an attorney attempts to question you about reports you prepared, always ask to see the report. Read it, be sure it is your signature, and be sure everything in it can be attributed to you. If it is not your signature or writing, do not take responsibility for it. If it is your report, the attorney may use it to undermine your current testimony.

He may attempt to set you up as follows:

Q. You prepared this report immediately after the incident. Correct?

A. Yes.

Q. It's fair to say your memory was clearer at that time than it is now, two years later. Correct?

A. Yes.

Q. Yet you left out an important fact in your report. How do you explain that?

If there is not an obvious, truthful explanation, do not search for one. Do not speculate how the omission could have occurred. Moreover, if appropriate, do not concede that an error was made. You could say, if accurate, "The report was a summary, which I prepared in a few minutes. It does not contain everything that occurred."

The attorney may ask you to clarify what was inaccurate about the report. He may attempt to use the report to induce you to volunteer information, to speculate, or render opinions. Typically, the attorney might ask, "Why don't you read it through to yourself, and if you get to a sentence that you think is inaccurate or should be expanded on or if you want to make any comment regarding it, why don't you just indicate and tell us what you have in mind?"

Do not engage in this exercise. Answer, "I'm not sure I can do that correctly. If you want, I'll tell you what I saw and heard, and you can decide whether it's summarized in the report or not."

The foregoing recommendations neither cover every situation a witness may encounter nor provide responses for every type of questioning, but they should alert a witness to the difficulties he or she may face during a deposition. They should better a witness' understanding of the need for preparation, prudence, and humility.

Chapter Six

Understanding the Complexities of the Questioning Process

In courtroom trials, as an attorney is questioning a witness, his adversary can object to the question. When this occurs, the witness should not answer until the judge rules on the objection. If the judge sustains the objection, the witness does not have to answer the question. If the judge overrules the objection, the witness must answer.

In depositions, this familiar procedure is not followed. Since a judge is not present to immediately rule on objections, other types of procedures are employed. Objections to form, reserved objections, and objections on substantive evidentiary grounds are used in deposition practice.

Objections to Form

Objections to form must be raised or they are waived. These are objections to improper questions that can be corrected immediately. Grounds for objections can be that the questions are leading, compound, confusing, argumentative, misquote testimony, or assume facts not in evidence.

Counsel for the witness must object to the question as soon as it is asked so that the other attorney can withdraw, rephrase, or correct the question. If the witness' counsel neglects to raise an objection, the grounds for the objection are waived. Consequently, the question and answer could be admitted into evidence at the trial, despite the fact that the question may have been improper.

An objection to the form of the question should alert the witness that the posed question could be improper or difficult to answer, and the witness should be especially careful while doing so. If appropriate, he should ask for clarification or ask that the question be repeated or simply reply, "I don't understand the question."

Reserved Objections

Reserved objections, unlike objections to form, are objections to questions that violate the substantive rules of evidence. Such questions may violate the rules of evidence because they ask for testimony that is irrelevant, immaterial, incompetent, or they call for inadmissible hearsay, inadmissible opinion, or speculative answers. Such questions may broach recognized privileges, such as the attorney-client, doctor-patient or husband-wife privileges.

Reserved objections do not have to be raised by the attorneys during the deposition, but will be ruled on at a later time by the judge. The attorneys stipulate to this practice before the deposition and the stipulation will be included in the transcript; however, it is generally not explained to the witness.

A standard stipulation will read:

> IT IS HEREBY STIPULATED AND AGREED BY the attorneys for the parties hereto that:
>
> All rights provided by the Civil Practice Law and Rules, including the right to object to any question, except as to form, or to move to strike any testimony at this examination is reserved. And, in addition, the failure to object to any question or to move to strike testimony at this examination shall not be a bar or waiver to make such motion at, and is reserved for, trial of this action.

This practice has evolved because the courts do not want the deposition sessions to become bogged down with legal wrangling. Arguments over whether a question or series of questions should be admissible can be complex, and the judge may not be able to render an instant ruling. These issues may require the submission of written motions and memoranda of law. Consequently, judges encourage the parties to proceed with the deposition as far as possible and to resolve sticking points later.

This does not help the witness during the questioning. Not being aware that a privilege applies or not knowing the rules of evidence, the witness may answer questions that he would not have to answer at a trial. It is little consolation that the answers may be stricken at a later time. The witness still undergoes the questioning, and his answers may lead to other areas of inquiry. Clearly, a witness at a deposition is in a far more difficult position than a witness in a regular courtroom trial.

Police officers, generally, cannot be expected to have a perfect knowledge of the rules of evidence, but a basic working knowledge can be extremely helpful to them. If a question sounds as though it is something that would be inadmissible at a trial, such as hearsay or privileged information, the officer should be cautious about answering the question.

If a witness expects questions about areas of privacy, such as employment or health records, he should discuss the issue with his counsel beforehand. Armed with foreknowledge, the counsel may be able to obtain protective orders to prevent questioning into private matters.

Objections Raised on Substantive Evidentiary Grounds

When the question by an examining attorney raises a substantive issue, such as the privilege of protected employment records, the counsel for the witness may choose not to rely on the reserved objections but instead may choose to immediately voice an objection.

After objecting, the counsel for the witness may choose either to allow the witness to answer or to direct him not to answer. In the first instance, the witness, despite the objection, must still give an answer as shown in the following example:

Q. Other than this occasion, during your career as a police officer, did you ever discharge your service revolver in the line of duty?

Witness' counsel: "Objection, you can answer."

A. The only time in my career was the incident, which is at hand.

In the second instance in which the counsel directs the witness not to answer, it is not uncommon for the attorneys to battle one another. Not answering a question goes against the tenor of the discovery statutes, but the counsel for the witness might believe it would be too damaging to allow the witness to answer. The examining attorney may ignore the objection and tell the witness, "You may answer." If counsel for the witness still refuses to let the witness answer, the examining attorney may stop the proceedings to contact the judge for a ruling. The judge may give an immediate ruling or reserve his ruling and advise the attorneys to skip the debated questions for now and to proceed with the remainder of the deposition. The following is an example of the witness' counsel not permitting an answer:

Q. You did not voluntarily resign from the police department, correct?

Witness' counsel: Objection, directing him not to answer.

Q. From the time of your admission to the department until the day of your termination, were there ever any disciplinary complaints filed against you by the department?

Witness' counsel: Objection, don't answer.

Q. Are you directing him not to answer?

Witness' counsel: Yes.

Q. During the same period of time, did you ever have alcohol or drug-related rehabilitation while employed with the department?

Witness' counsel: Objection, directing him not to answer.

These questions raised the issue of privileged employment records, and the judge would have to make a legal ruling as to whether they were relevant and whether the value of the information outweighed any privacy concerns. Discovery rules lean toward unearthing information rather than privacy considerations, and in the majority of such cases, judges direct the witness to answer. If the judge directs the witness to answer and the witness refuses, the witness and his counsel can be subject to sanctions. In most states the discovery rules are quite broad. In Federal courts, the rules are broader, and an attorney who instructs his client not to answer a question on grounds of irrelevancy risks sanctioning by the court. The Federal Rules of Civil Procedure allow questions related to "any matter, not privileged, which is relevant to the subject matter involved in the pending action."[1] Even if the information sought will not be admissible at trial, it will be allowed at deposition, "If the information sought appears reasonably calculated to lead to the discovery of admissible evidence."[2] Under federal rules, a witness' counsel who instructs the witness not to answer on grounds of irrelevancy must make a motion to the court for a ruling.[3] Instructing the witness to not answer cannot be used as an informal tactic to thwart the inquiry. This is yet another example of how a deposition witness is not in an advantageous position and can be pressed to divulge information far beyond what he would have to divulge at a trial.

---

1. *Federal Rules of Civil Procedure*, Section (26)(b)(1).
2. Id.
3. *Federal Rules of Civil Procedure*, Section (30)(d).

Opinions-Speculations-Assumptions-Conclusions

As a general rule of evidence, ordinary witnesses cannot testify to their opinions, and their testimony should be restricted to what they know first-hand, based on their sight, hearing, smell, taste, or touch. They must testify to facts, not to their opinions drawn from the facts. It is the role of judge or jury to make inferences and draw conclusions based on the facts to which the witness testifies. However, these general statements must be further clarified. When people describe what they observed, of necessity they include common approximations, assessments, and opinions. When describing the speed of a moving vehicle, they do not state the exact amount of time it took the vehicle to move from point A to point B. They give an approximation, such as, about fifty miles per hour. When identifying a person as the person seen on a previous occasion, witnesses do not describe every contour of the person's body and face but state that in their opinion it is the same person. When identifying the signature of someone they know, they do not describe all the handwriting characteristics they observed but simply identify the signature. When describing a person's apparent emotional state, they do not describe every physical manifestation—they state that the person appeared agitated, calm, happy, or depressed.

Aside from these common opinions that are necessary for everyday communication, ordinary witnesses should not be allowed to give opinion testimony that requires knowledge or expertise beyond that of an average person. They cannot give opinion testimony about the ultimate questions to be decided by the judge or jury. They cannot give conclusive legal opinions about guilt, liability, negligence, recklessness, or whether safety standards or proper procedures were violated.

In contrast to ordinary witnesses, expert witnesses who are deemed qualified by the court can provide opinion evidence that depends on professional or scientific knowledge or skill not within the range of the ordinary training or intelligence of average citizens.[4] For instance, qualified experts can give their opinions whether fingerprints left at a crime scene match the fingerprints of a suspect, whether a person died of natural causes or as a result of a homicidal act, whether a vehicle accident was caused by mechanical failure, or whether a person was mentally competent to stand trial.

---

4. *Dougherty v. Milliken*, 163 NY 527, 533 (1900).

At depositions, the rules regarding opinion evidence are relaxed, and ordinary witnesses are often asked to give opinions or to speculate. The purpose of the relaxed rules is to facilitate the discovery of relevant evidence, and attorneys use the leeway they have to get the witness talking, to pressure him, and to manipulate him into giving answers he had not planned to give. The attorney may ask a police officer questions about legal conclusions, or ask him to speculate about why other officers took certain actions. The attorney may begin the questions as follows:

"Officer, Isn't it possible that … ?"

"Wouldn't it be fair to say that … ?"

"Can't we safely theorize that … ?"

"Isn't it just as likely that … ?"

"Isn't it logical to infer that … ?"

The witness' counsel should object to these types of questions, because they call for inadmissible opinions, conclusions, and speculation. Nevertheless, the witness may be directed to answer. If the witness answers, he should avoid saying, "Anything is possible," or "Maybe."

Rather he could answer, "I don't know."

If the attorney persists, he could then say, "And I don't think I should speculate." Questions that call for answers based on hearsay are inadmissible at trial unless an exception applies. However, during depositions, questions calling for hearsay are permissible because they may lead to the discovery of relevant evidence. For example, a witness may not know through his own observation that a particular police supervisor was present during an incident, but he may testify that he heard the supervisor was present during the incident. This discovered information could be the basis for the examining attorney to subpoena the supervisor and question him about his observations and knowledge.

Cross-examination Despite Objections

While deposing a police officer-witness, the examining attorney, despite objections, might persistently ask leading questions. He might persist even though he knows that the questions and answers obtained will not be available for use at trial. This circumstance may arise when the attorney senses that he can undermine a key witness so thoroughly that the opposing side will be forced to settle. For the witness, the deposition can become a harrowing experience. Unless the witness has the facts on his side or is extremely adept at handling aggressive questioning, he is likely to suffer serious setbacks to his position.

In a New York City case of false arrest and negligent investigation filed in federal court, the plaintiff had been arrested for a robbery that occurred in an elevator. He was arrested after the victim picked out his photograph from police arrest photographs and subsequently identified him in a lineup. The plaintiff was held in jail for nine months until his trial. When the trial began, the victim left the country and the case against the plaintiff was dismissed. He sued the police for violation of his civil rights, false arrest, and negligent investigation, claiming that his arrest was not justified because the identification procedures employed were not proper and the police did not interview other witnesses.

During the deposition of the investigating detective, the examining attorney disregarded the objections to his leading questions in order to obtain the answers he wanted regarding the detective's failure to interview two potential witnesses.

Q. Your testimony is that the female witness would not be of any assistance, is that correct?

A. That's correct.

Q. That's an assumption that you are making looking back over this case, is that correct?

A. That's correct.

Q. You knew that the witness was on the elevator with the perpetrator, is that right?

A. At one time, she was on the elevator with the perpetrator, but she did not see the crime.

Q. I didn't ask you whether she saw the crime. You knew that she was on the elevator with the perpetrator, is that right?

A. Yes.

Q. And you knew she had at least two conversations with the perpetrator, is that right?

A. Yes.

Q. It would be fair to assume that she was probably looking at him when she was having these conversations, is that right?

A. No.

Q. It's not fair to assume that?

A. When you say, it's fair to assume that she is looking, I could be speaking to you and looking at someone else.

Q. Right. But one way we could clarify this, Detective, if you had interviewed the witness.

Witness' Counsel: Objection.

Q. Is that right? That would clarify my question, wouldn't it?

Counsel: Objection again.

A. There is no document that I had down that I interviewed her, that's correct.

Q. But my question for you right at this point is not about a document. My question for you that we have sitting here today is a question as to whether the witness looked at this perpetrator, is that right?

A. Yes.

Q. And the reason we have this question is because you didn't interview the witness, is that right?

Counsel: Objection.

A. That's correct.

Q. And had you interviewed her, for all you know, she would have told you, I got a good look at him.

Counsel: Objection.

Q. Is that right?

A. That's correct.

Q. You never spoke to this woman?

A. That's correct.

Q. And you never spoke to the man on the first floor, who let this guy into the building either, is that right?

A. That's correct.

Q. Why didn't you speak to either of these witnesses?

A. The man did not see the crime.

Q. You knew he lived on the first floor.

A. That's correct.

Q. You knew he had a conversation with the perpetrator of first degree robbery?

A. (No verbal response).

Q. Right?

A. There was a person who spoke to the alleged perpetrator, yes.

Q. Admittedly, it was before the robbery took place.

A. Yes.

Q. But within moments of the robbery taking place, is that right?

A. Yes.

Q. Help me again. Why didn't you speak to this man on the first floor?

A. He did not see the crime.

Q. But he did see the perpetrator, is that right?

A. According to the witness.

Q. He saw the perpetrator, is that right?

A. (Nods head affirmatively).

Q. I'm sorry. You have to answer.

A. Yes.

Q. As a detective, it is not your position that a proper investigation means you only interview witnesses to the crime, is it?

Counsel: Objection to the form.

Q. Is it?

A. (No verbal response).

Q. A prudent detective interviews witnesses who can identify criminals.

Counsel: Objection.

Q. A prudent detective interviews witnesses who can identify a criminal even if they haven't seen the actual crime, is that correct?

Counsel: Objection.

Q. Let me ask you this: Do you think it's reasonable that you didn't speak to the man on the first floor as you sit here today?

A. I did not speak to him. I have no knowledge that I spoke to him.

Q. Is that reasonable in your view?

Counsel: Objection to the form.

A. I can't give you a concrete answer why he wasn't spoken to before.

Q. I'm not asking you why.

A. Listen to me. It could have been …

Q. I'm asking you, is it reasonable?

Counsel: I object to the form of the question.

Q. Is it reasonable that you didn't speak to the man on the first floor, Detective?

A. At the time of the incident when I started the investigation, there's a reason possibly why I didn't speak to him.

Q. But you don't know that, is that right?

A. I don't know that because I don't have it documented. That's correct.

Q. What was the reason that you never interviewed the man downstairs?

A. I don't know right now.

Q. You can't explain it.

A. No.

Q. What, if anything, did you do to follow up this lead of the man who let the robbery perpetrator into the building?

A. I don't recall.

Q. As you sit here today, you can't say even that you did anything, can you?

Counsel: Objection to the form.

Q. Can you?

A. I don't recall what was done.

Q. Do you recall anything at all?

Counsel: Objection to the form. He just testified he doesn't remember.

Q. Now, I'm asking a follow-up question, which is: Do you recall having done anything at all?

A. For some reason, I don't know what it was or why it was, I didn't interview that man.

Q. You could have if you wanted to, is that right?

A. He could have left the country the next day.

Q. When you say 'He could have…,' I don't want you testifying about what could have been that you have no basis to believe actually was. If you wanted to, you had plenty of opportunity to interview this man, didn't you?

Counsel: Objection to the form.

A. (No verbal response).

Q. In other words, you were not sick, you were not in a hospital or anything like that.

A. I was not, no.

Q. So, if you wanted to, you could have gone to this building and spoken to this man, couldn't you?

A. I guess so.

The examining attorney maintained the intensity of the questioning for more than seven hours. The detective's answers to the majority of the questions posed were comparable to those cited above. He tried to fend off the onslaught of questions, but he succeeded only in supporting the plaintiff's claim that the investigation was lacking. Toward the end of the deposition, the attorney returned to the subject of why the detective did not interview the female witness, and confronted the detective with his prior testimony at a *Wade* hearing.

Q. When I asked you earlier today why the witness did not view the lineup, you told me that you had made a determination that she had no value for this case; is that right?

A. Yes.

Q. (Handing document). Do you recognize this to be a transcript of your testimony in the *Wade* hearing?

A. Yes.

Q. What I would like you to do, please, is read it. Then I will read portions and then ask some questions. Do you understand?

A. Okay.

Q. (Reading).

   The Court: Did you get a name for this woman?

   Witness: I was given her name by the complainant.

   The Court: Did you ever ask her to look at the lineup?

   Witness: No. I didn't have an opportunity to get her.

   Court: Did you try to get her?

   Witness: No, I didn't because I was in a rush to do the lineup, but due to overtime, I just went to get the complainant.

Q. Was that your testimony?

A. Yes.

Q. When I asked you earlier today why the witness did not view the lineup, you didn't say anything about overtime? What you told me is that you had made a determination that she had no value to this case; is that right?

A. Yes.

Q. Having read this testimony, what is the reason you didn't have her do the lineup? Was it because you didn't think she was of any value or because you were concerned about overtime?

Counsel: Objection to the form.

A. I think it was both.

Q. What was your concern with respect to overtime?

A. Because I was in a rush to get this done.

Q. Did they want you to rush through the lineup?

A. They want us to conduct it as fast as possible.

Q. But you said you were in a rush; is that right?

A. I think I exaggerated a little bit when I gave that answer.

Q. But your answer didn't say anything about having made a decision that the witness was of no investigative value. did you?

A. No.

The results of this deposition might have been avoided had the counsel for the witness objected to the leading questions and called the judge for a ruling ordering the plaintiff's attorney to desist from conducting the deposition in a cross-examination format. Even without such a ruling, the detective should not have engaged the leading questions, especially those for which his counsel placed an objection to the form of the question on the record. Many of the questions called for assumptions or unsupported conclusions, and the detective did not recall the details of the case. He should have answered the leading questions with a simple "I don't recall" or "I don't know," instead of speculating as to what occurred.

Lost in the argument was the ultimate issue of whether the plaintiff did, in fact, commit the robbery. It was never disproved, and it was not established that the police acted without probable cause. The victim identified the plaintiff as the person who robbed her, and she testified in the grand jury. Unfortunately, however, she left the country and failed to appear at the trial, which resulted in the dismissal of the criminal charges. Her failure to follow through on her complaint opened the door for the lawsuit and the attempt to shift the blame for the inconclusive court proceedings to the police department.

CHAPTER SEVEN

Circumstances Conducive to Lawsuits

Repeated errors and omissions that occur during law-enforcement activities become the predicates for lawsuits against the police. Nearly every lawsuit against the police incorporates one of the following circumstances: unnecessary dismissal of criminal charges, inconsistent police testimony, inaccurate written reports, or mishandling of records. Police departments should take measures to lessen the recurrences of these errors and omissions.

Dismissal of Criminal Charges

When criminal charges are dismissed before trial or after an acquittal, the door opens for civil charges against the police for false arrest, malicious prosecution, unlawful imprisonment, violation of civil rights, and if physical force was employed, assault and battery.

This is an area where law-enforcement officers create potential lawsuits against themselves and their agencies. They allow a case to be dismissed, not because it should be, but because the officer, or his supervisors, or the district attorneys are not paying enough attention. It seems they do not foresee the possible consequences.

Officers often fail to make court appearances, to prepare and keep complete records, find and interview witnesses, gather and preserve all the evidence, or articulate sufficient grounds for probable cause. In domestic violence situations, the police frequently make an arrest for assault or other charges based on the complaint of a family member, spouse, or partner. To accomplish the arrest the police may have to use a certain amount of force because the defendant is emotionally distraught, resistant, or unruly. The police, not wanting to be involved in a domestic violence matter, fail to add the charges of resisting arrest, menacing, or attempted assault against the officer. In the event that the complainant does not follow through in court, the underlying charges will be dismissed, opening the possibility of a suit for the defendant's incarceration and any physical or psychological injuries sustained.

Police supervisors for the most part are unaware of the manner in which individual arrest cases are handled in criminal court. Traditionally, the policy of most departments has been to keep their distance from the court process based on the rationale that oversight of officers during their courtroom testimony might appear as undue pressure to obtain a high conviction rate. This lack of supervision and support of arresting officers at a critical time when they could benefit from instruction and training by experienced supervisors leads to dismissals of viable cases.

With respect to arrests, some police supervisors tend to think that their job is limited to ensuring that prisoners are expeditiously processed and delivered to the court, and their concerns may relate more to minimizing overtime costs than helping to ensure that the arrests will stand up. Supervisors regularly send one officer to process several prisoners, an action that can come back to haunt the supervisor if he later becomes a defendant in a lawsuit because the charges were dismissed.

A common example is the assignment of several prisoners arrested at a brawl or demonstration to an officer who does not have firsthand knowledge of the alleged actions and crimes of each prisoner. When the officer appears in court, he may tell the district attorney preparing the complaint something to the effect: "I only arrested the guy because the sergeant told me to. It was a big demonstration. Things were getting out of control, so they wanted to make arrests."

Another common example is a narcotics raid after which the arresting officer may tell the district attorney, "We rounded up a lot of suspects and the boss told me they were all acting in concert."

In some instances the arrests may be for relatively minor charges, such as disorderly conduct, harassment, simple assault, criminal mischief, possession of small amounts of narcotics, and the district attorney may be busy with other more important cases. He may conclude that the police have not presented a good case and there is not much he can do to prevent a dismissal or an acquittal. The district attorney may not try hard enough to get the supervisor or other officers to sign supporting depositions, and, consequently, the case may be dismissed.

Many police officers and supervisors do not fully appreciate the importance of convictions and establishing probable cause. In cases in which the police used force to make an arrest and a court subsequently determines that there was insufficient probable cause for the arrest, the force that the police used will be deemed unlawful. Necessary and justifiable force is transformed into civil assault and battery.

Furthermore, when a defendant is charged with resisting arrest in addition to the initial offense, probable cause for the initial arrest must be established for the resisting arrest charge to be valid. New York State's statute is typical of most states:

> A person is guilty of resisting arrest when he intentionally prevents or attempts to prevent a police officer or peace officer from effecting an authorized arrest of himself or another person.[1]

To be found guilty, the defendant's initial arrest must have been "authorized." Therefore, it is imperative that the police obtain, document, and preserve evidence to support the initial charge. They cannot rely on the defendant's resistance as a basis for a lawful arrest.

A dismissal of a criminal case does not automatically mean that the plaintiff will win a civil lawsuit, but it greatly increases his chances. The lawyer will surely go before the jury and say that the criminal court exonerated his client. He will argue, "They did not think he should have been arrested, charged, and subjected to assault and battery, neither should you."

Suspect Killed by Police

In cases involving shootings or other force used by police officers that result in the death of a suspect, the police department will conduct an investigation of the officer's actions to determine whether the officer acted lawfully and within the parameters of proper police conduct. However, the department investigation, focusing on the conduct of the officer, often neglects to fully identify, collect, develop, and preserve evidence regarding the conduct of the deceased suspect. Since the suspect is dead, no arrest or prosecution will follow. Without a need to present evidence to support an arrest or prosecution, the incentive is lacking to develop and prove the suspect's guilt beyond a reasonable doubt. The investigation does not fully focus on the actions of the suspect as it would in a case in which the officer had been killed and the suspect had been arrested and charged with his murder.

When the preliminary investigation indicates that the actions of the officer were justified, for example, in self-defense, the district attorney will either

---

1. *NY Penal Law*, Section 205.30.

decline to prosecute or will present the facts to a grand jury. If the grand jury exonerates the officer, the police department will most likely close their administrative investigation.

Exoneration of an officer of criminal or administrative charges pertaining to the death does not preclude a civil lawsuit for wrongful death or violation of civil rights by the decedent's family. Often in these lawsuits, the plaintiffs' attorney can exploit the lack of developed proof of criminal conduct by the decedent.

In a Bronx, New York, case an officer shot and killed a drug dealer who allegedly had wrestled the officer's service revolver away from him. The officer pulled his backup gun and shot the drug dealer, who died immediately. Police investigating supervisors immediately responded to the scene of the shooting. They saw the condition of the officer who had been engaged in a vicious punching and wrestling fight with the drug dealer. The officer was shaken and injured. The drug dealer lay in the street with the officer's service revolver at his side. The investigating supervisors accepted the officer's account that the drug dealer had wrestled his gun from him. It was an open and shut case. Their investigation found that the officer's actions were justified, and, subsequently, the grand jury exonerated the officer, voting no true bill. Nevertheless, the decedent's family sued, claiming the officer unnecessarily shot the decedent and there was no proof, other than the officer's word, that the decedent had taken his gun.[2]

The plaintiffs' attorney exploited the fact that the investigators failed to examine the officer's service revolver for the suspect's fingerprints. The defending attorney, knowing that a jury would expect the police to have conducted a full investigation, including taking fingerprints, was placed in a difficult position. Although she may have explained to the jury that fingerprints are rarely recovered from guns because a well-oiled gun obscures fingerprints and the movement that occurs when a gun is fired or handled tends to smudge fingerprints, the jurors would still surely ask, why not try. For this reason, among others, the city was forced to pay a lucrative settlement.

The police investigators should have conducted the investigation as though the officer had been killed and the drug dealer had to be prosecuted without the officer available to testify against him. A full-scale crime-scene search for fingerprint, blood, and other trace evidence should have been conducted. Witnesses from the scene should have been interviewed and their

---

2. *Nelson v. City of New York*, NY Supreme Court (Bronx, Ct.Rpt.Bowles, 1992).

interviews videotaped. Witnesses regarding the drug dealer's background and activities should have been found and interviewed. If necessary, search warrants to obtain evidence pertinent to the drug dealer's activities and his motivations should have been obtained.

All incidents in which suspects are killed by the police must be investigated to the same extent that would occur had the suspect survived and been prosecuted.

Conflicting Police Testimony

Plaintiff attorneys thrive on conflicting police testimony, whether officers contradict one another or an officer contradicts himself. Even contradictions regarding relatively minor matters raise the specter of lying, and lying raises the specter of conspiracy. If a lawyer can convince a jury that the police engaged in a conspiracy to injure the plaintiff or to cover up police misconduct, large monetary awards will follow.

An inordinate number of conflicts arise in police testimony. They arise partly because of the restrictions on normal communication after controversial police incidents. This lack of communication can be attributed to two important reasons. One, officers want to avoid allegations by attorneys that they conspired to invent a story. Two, many controversial cases potentially involve criminal charges and officers are instructed by their union delegates and attorneys not to discuss the case. Criminal charges against the police are filed infrequently, but the potential for such charges is a constant, and a competent attorney must advise his clients not to discuss a potential criminal case with anyone because the person they talk with could become a witness against them.

This criminal-case mentality adversely affects civil-lawsuit defense. Although plaintiffs and their witnesses hold meetings with their attorneys to discuss testimony and plan strategies from the outset, police-officer defendants stay at arms length from one another. This arms-length posture maintains itself even after the district attorney or the grand jury determines that there will not be a criminal prosecution.

In cases that are not going to be prosecuted criminally, officers should be able to have normal discussions. It is perfectly natural for people to talk about an unusual or critical event. As long as officers do not change their testimony from what they believe is truthful and do not conspire to give identical testimony, they can exchange information and viewpoints. Open discussion can uncover discrepancies, can correct an officer whose testimony would have been inaccurate or patently false, and can refresh an officer's recollection. Nevertheless, many officers avoid discussing the case with other officers because of a general belief that it is not appropriate. This lack of communication leaves officers inadequately prepared during civil lawsuits.

An example of contradictory testimony from two radio car partners occurred in a lawsuit brought on behalf of an off-duty sanitation worker who had been killed in an automobile collision. The plaintiffs alleged that a police vehicle chase resulted in the collision in which the decedent was killed. The two police officers denied they were chasing a vehicle but claimed they heard the collision and responded to render aid. During their depositions, officer A described what happened when they responded, as follows:

Q: What was the next thing that you did as you were approaching the scene?

A: Just when I got to the scene and I got out of my vehicle we put on the lights, our turret lights.

Q: What happened then?

A: I got out of my vehicle. From what I remember, there was a male, white, that was on the street. He was sitting down on the street. I remember he was mumbling something. I said, "Lay back down. Stay still."

Q: When you first saw the white man that was injured in the accident, was he already out of his car?

A: From what I remember, he was already out of his car, yes.

Q: What happened then?

A: Just then the units started to arrive. Fire Department came. EMS came. Other units.

Q: Were you the ones first at the scene, to the best of your knowledge, after the accident?

A: Yes.

Officer B, the partner of officer A, testified quite differently.

Q: What did you see as you got closer to the scene of the accident?

A: We saw the aftermath of the collision.

Q: What was the next thing that you did?

A: We pulled the sanitation worker out.

Q: Did both you and your partner get out of your squad car?

A: Yes.

Q: Do you remember what you did?

A: I remember helping - I remember us pulling that sanitation worker out.

Q: Can you tell me what you did to get him out of the car?

A: Don't recall specifically but it didn't take a lot, wasn't like pinned or trapped. I just remember pulling him and he came freely.

Although this testimony did not go directly to the issue of whether the officers had been chasing a vehicle, it was contradictory. Such contradictory testimony can be attributed to faulty memories or to deceit. If a jury believes the latter, they may conclude that an officer who lied about one fact, lied about everything.

Had there been proper preparation and communication between the officers, the contradiction could have been brought to the attention of the attorney. Contradictions can arise from differing perspectives or assumptions, and may be explainable. It is better to acknowledge that contradictions exist and present them with their explanations than to allow the opposing attorney to uncover and expose them.

Inaccurate Official Reports

For important police incidents, such as a police shooting, superior officers prepare preliminary but official reports. Inaccuracies, discrepancies, or unsupported conclusions in these reports can become useful ammunition for plaintiff attorneys. Superior officers responsible for preparing preliminary reports should stick to the known facts and avoid speculation or unnecessary conclusions. Typically, after a police shooting, superior officers conduct an immediate investigation under time-pressure conditions because the police chief will demand a report as soon as possible so he can brief the mayor or issue a press release. However, the superior officers investigating the incident will not be able to interview the officer who fired his weapon. Department rules or contractual agreements may preclude interviewing the officer for a certain period of time. The more important reason for not conducting an interview is that a shooting is potentially a crime, and the officer has the constitutional right to remain silent. If the department forces the officer to answer questions under threat of terminating his employment, any answer given by the officer would be inadmissible against him in a criminal court and, in addition, any evidence derived from his answers might be inadmissible under the fruits of the poisonous tree doctrine. Therefore, the district attorney generally advises the police department not to conduct an interview until a decision is made whether or not to prosecute the officer.

Without a statement from the officer, the investigators often have difficulty ascertaining the facts of what occurred. Nevertheless, they will prepare the most comprehensive report they can. To do this, they may rely on secondhand information or inferences, which can lead to an inaccurate and misleading report.

Investigating officers should abide by rules that give an officer time to confer with an attorney before answering questions. They should not solicit off-the-cuff statements. They should avoid including hearsay accounts or unverified statements in the preliminary report, although such information should be preserved in the case file.

A preliminary report was used in a lawsuit against the police in 2003, when a Bronx, New York, jury found an officer liable for shooting a man holding a knife. The officer and his partner had answered a call from two people that a man had chased and threatened them. While searching for the man, the officers were near an elevator when its door suddenly opened. The first officer found himself face to face with the man, while his partner was on the other side of the opened door and could not see what transpired. The first officer shot and wounded the man. Subsequently, the man was acquitted of criminal charges and sued the police. At the civil trial, the first officer testified that the plaintiff had a large butcher knife at his side and was moving toward him. However, the initial incident report prepared by supervisors on the night of the shooting contradicted the officer's account. Although the supervisors had not officially interviewed either the officer or his partner, the partner in an off-the-cuff exchange had indicated to one of the supervisors that the plaintiff had a large knife. He made this indication by holding his hands up a distance apart to illustrate the large size of the knife. The supervisor interpreted the hand movement to mean that the plaintiff had held the knife over his head. This interpretation was incorrectly included in the incident report, and was relied on by the plaintiff's attorney to imply that the police had initially tried to frame the plaintiff with the false story that he had raised the knife over his head in a threatening manner.

The jury awarded the plaintiff a large sum of money. Whether the jury would have held for the plaintiff regardless of the contradictory report will never be clear. Undoubtedly, the inconsistent police versions played into the attorney's theme of police cover-up, conspiracy, and the ever-popular blue wall of silence. This result was entirely avoidable. The elevator door had blocked the partner's view, and he could not have seen the plaintiff's movements before the shooting. The partner's hand movements in describing the size of the knife were, in effect, an unverified hearsay statement, which should not have been included in the supervisor's report.

In another New York City case, preliminary police reports jeopardized a police officer's defense. The officer, with his sergeant, was working anti-crime patrol in plainclothes in an unmarked vehicle. Both officers observed a man looking into vehicles in a suspicious manner. When they attempted to stop and question him, the suspect ran. The police officer got out of his car and chased the suspect approximately two blocks while the sergeant followed in the vehicle. The chase proceeded into a backyard, and believing the suspect was armed with a gun, the officer shot him. Seconds after the shooting, the sergeant arrived in the backyard, and the officer briefly told him what happened. The suspect died immediately and lay face up on the ground. He had an apparent bullet wound to his upper abdomen. He did not have a gun.

A lieutenant arrived on the scene and the sergeant advised him what had occurred. When the crime-scene unit arrived, they took photographs of the body and conducted a search for physical evidence.

During the initial investigation, the police inspector conducting the investigation did not interview the officer, but he did interview the sergeant and the lieutenant. On the basis of those interviews and the report from the crime-scene unit, the inspector prepared a report indicating that the suspect had been shot once in the chest and that the officer had told the sergeant that he fired because the suspect had "turned around, he was crouching, he had a gun."

The lieutenant prepared an additional report in which he indicated the officer fired from a distance of about five feet because "the perpetrator turned around into an apparent combat stance."

Based on the account that the suspect had turned toward the officer and had a bullet wound in the front of his body, the inspector's report indicated the officer had shot the suspect as the suspect faced him.

The Medical Examiner's report contradicted these preliminary police reports. The wound in the torso was an exit wound, not an entrance wound. The medical examiner found a single bullet "entered the right-side of (the decedent's) lower back, and exited through the upper right-side of his abdomen." Moreover, the physical evidence indicated that the shooting occurred from a greater distance than five feet since no gun powder residue was found on the decedent's clothing and the officer's spent shell casing was recovered twenty-five feet from the body.

Later, during the investigation, the officer testified before the Grand Jury, the Civilian Complaint Review Board, and the police department. In his accounts, he consistently testified that he fired his weapon from twenty-five to thirty feet. The suspect had not turned and taken a combat stance, but had partially turned while running and extended his right arm. The officer believed he saw an object in the suspect's hand, and that was why he fired.

The officer's account was consistent with the physical evidence and the bullet entrance wound in the lower back. Although he was mistaken about the suspect having a gun, the grand jury determined that under the circumstances, the officer acted in accordance with a reasonable belief, and they did not indict him.

Nevertheless, the inconsistencies in the police reports provided extensive inflammatory material on which to bring a civil lawsuit for wrongful death. The inspector's report relied on the information provided by the lieutenant, which relied on the information provided by the sergeant of what he thought the police officer had said immediately after the shooting. The multiple layers of hearsay established a version of the incident that proved to be inconsistent with the officer's later testimony. Under these circumstances, the inevitable lawsuit was filed.

Records as Weapons

In criminal cases, the prosecution must turn over police records, notes, and prior witness statements to the defendant. In New York this rule, emanating from *People v. Rosario*,[3] is especially stringent in that a failure to do so, even when the failure amounts to a harmless error, requires an automatic reversal of a conviction.[4]

Criminal defendants whose convictions are reversed become eligible to file lawsuits against the police as occurred in the case of Richard Moore, who later changed his name to Dhoruba Bin Wahad.

Bin Wahad was a member of the Black Liberation Army (BLA), a branch of the Black Panther Party, a radical political group that advocated various violent forms of political revolution. One of the goals of the BLA was to kill police officers, especially black and white police teams.

---

3. *People v. Rosario*, 9 NY 2d 286 (1961).
4. *People v. Ranghelle*, 69 NY 2d 56 (1986).

On May 19, 1971, two police officers, Thomas Curry and Nicholas Binetti, were parked on Riverside Drive, in New York City, guarding the house of the New York County District Attorney, Frank Hogan, whose life had been threatened by the Black Panthers. The officers observed a blue Maverick sedan going the wrong way on a one-way street, gave chase, and pulled alongside the car at Riverside Drive and West 106th Street. As they did, an occupant of the car fired a .45 caliber machine gun at the officers, severely wounding both of them.

On May 21, 1971, two police officers, Waverly Jones and Joseph Piagentini answered a 911 call at a housing development in Harlem. As they walked back to their patrol car, two young men took out guns and shot them in the back. Jones was shot once in the back of the head and three times in the spine. He died quickly. Piagentini lived a little longer. The youths turned him over and shot him several more times. In all he was shot thirteen times, and he died on the way to Harlem Hospital.

On May 21, 1971, a package was delivered to the *New York Times*, and a similar package was delivered to radio station WLIB. Each package contained a license plate from the car used in the shooting of Curry and Binetti, a .45 caliber bullet, and a revolutionary message from the BLA.

The following day, on May 22, 1971, a second message was received at the *New York Times* in which the BLA took credit for killing Jones and Piagentini. Subsequent laboratory tests proved that the messages were typed on the same typewriter. Bin Wahad's fingerprints were found on the first package sent to the *New York Times*.

On June 2, 1971, Bin Wahad, Eddie Josephs, and two other men, armed with several guns, attempted to rob the Triple O social club in the Bronx. During the robbery, the gunmen ordered the patrons to take off their clothes. One of the gunmen fired a shot, and someone alerted the police, who quickly responded. As the police surrounded the club, Bin Wahad ordered the patrons to put their clothes back on and walk out of the building. Mixing in with the patrons, the four robbers tried to get away but were caught by the police.

Police Officers Patrick Harnett, who later became the police chief of Hartford, Connecticut, and Thomas McCarron arrested Bin Wahad and Josephs. Inside the club, the officers recovered five guns and a .45 caliber machine gun. The machine gun was rushed to the ballistics laboratory and identified as the same weapon used in the May 19th shooting of Officers Curry and Binetti.

With news accounts connecting Wahad and Josephs to the murders of Curry and Binetti, the girlfriend of Eddie Josephs called a police hot line.

When detectives interviewed her, she attempted to extricate Josephs from any connection to the murders. She told the detectives that Bin Wahad and other BLA members had stayed with her and Josephs. She said that on May 19, 1971, the night of the shootings of Curry and Binetti, Josephs had stayed home with her while Bin Wahad and the others went out. When they came back, Bin Wahad asked her to help him clean out the blue Maverick sedan and she saw a machine gun in the car and spent bullet cartridges all over the floor.

The police searched her apartment and found the typewriter used for the two messages to the *New York Times*, Bin Wahad's fingerprints, and written materials that advocated killing police.

The FBI was also investigating the BLA in connection with numerous shootings of police across the country. The FBI and the NYPD conducted their investigations independently of each other. FBI agents interviewed the girlfriend three times and made summaries of her information. The FBI prepared a comprehensive report on the Black Panthers and the BLA, totaling 219 pages, seventeen of which pertained to the interviews with the girlfriend. They gave a copy of the report to the NYPD Chief of Detectives, Albert Seedman, for intelligence purposes. Chief Seedman kept the report in his safe and did not show it to anyone from the New York District Attorney's office.

Bin Wahad was convicted of the murders of Curry and Binetti, and sentenced to twenty-five years to life in prison. In addition, he pled guilty to an unrelated murder and was sentenced to seven years in prison, and he was also convicted of the Triple O robbery and sentenced to another seven years.

In spite of his criminal convictions, in 1975 Bin Wahad, with the aid of leftist political groups and radical-minded lawyers, sued the New York City Police Department, the New York State Department of Corrections, and the FBI for violating his civil rights.[5] During the discovery phase of the lawsuit, the federal judge ordered the NYPD and the FBI to turn over any documents related to investigations of Bin Wahad, the Black Panthers, or the BLA. The lawsuit stretched on for two decades, and, in all, more than 300,000 documents were turned over to Bin Wahad's attorneys. In 1988, the FBI turned over a copy of the 1971 report the FBI had given to Chief Seedman.

Armed with this newly discovered information obtained during the civil trial, Bin Wahad's attorneys filed a motion to vacate his murder convictions based on the *Rosario* grounds that the prosecution failed to turn over the in-

---

5. *Bin Wahad v. FBI, et al.*, US District Court, SDNY, 75 Civ. 6203 (1998).

formation in the report. The motion was brought even though the prosecution did not have any knowledge of the report.

The motion was denied by New York State Supreme Court Justice Peter McQuillan who ruled that although there was a *Rosario* violation, the conviction would stand. He ruled that the violation was only a harmless error since there was overwhelming evidence against Bin Wahad and the information would not have changed the outcome of the trial.

In 1993, McQuillan's ruling was overturned by the Appellate Division, which held that the harmless error doctrine could not be applied to any *Rosario* violation, under any circumstances. The Appellate Division ordered Bin Wahad's conviction vacated and granted him a new trial.[6]

The district attorney could not feasibly retry him. Almost twenty years had past. Witnesses were dead or not to be found. Memories had faded. Physical evidence had been discarded. As a result, Bin Wahad was released from prison.

Out of prison, his civil lawsuit picked up momentum and was expanded with added counts of malicious prosecution and withholding evidence. The agencies as defendants in the civil lawsuits suffered the same handicaps as the district attorney. They had not expected or prepared for a civil trial to go forward twenty years after the fact. Each of them settled, and the settlement totaled approximately one million dollars for Bin Wahad.

The simple lesson of this case for law enforcement is that accountability for records is of paramount importance, and records must be maintained even after criminal defendants are convicted. Convictions do not always stand, and the statute of limitations for filing a civil lawsuit begins when the criminal conviction is vacated. As a result, it is necessary for agencies to establish systems to locate records in their possession and to coordinate their record keeping with other agencies. District attorneys should notify municipal attorneys of appeals filed and convictions vacated, and, conversely, municipal attorneys should notify the district attorney when civil lawsuits are filed. All agencies should preserve records of any cases with a potential for further court proceedings.

A more sinister lesson for law-enforcement officers is that they must not underestimate the fanatical zeal of their adversaries. The Bin Wahad case was just one of many in which leftist political extremists joined forces with police-hating lawyers. What these two types have in common is that they will

---

6. *People v. Dhoruba Bin Wahad, fka Richard Moore*, 593 NYS 2d 939 (1993).

use and manipulate the rules of the legal system to turn the system upside down, either to defeat it or destroy it. Attacking the police, who, in their view, are instruments of an oppressive system, is a dramatic way to undermine the establishment. The extremists, by definition, do not subscribe to the tenets of the law and have no compunction about violating the law, including laws against perjury and false accusations. The police-hating lawyers will deny that the sanctions of the law should be applied to their clients, or themselves, but will stringently apply the technicalities of the law to the actions of the police.

New and Developing Theories of Liability

In recent years, a variety of novel theories to establish police liability have developed. One such theory is the state-created danger doctrine, which has been applied to a case in which demonstrators were attacked by a hostile crowd of onlookers. The theory rested on the assertion that the police at the scene, through inaction, communicated to the onlookers that they would not be arrested for misconduct toward the demonstrators.[7]

Police are also being sued in connection with domestic violence assaults. For example, when a woman makes a complaint to the police that her ex-husband had physically abused or threatened her, the police will file a report and advise the woman to obtain an order of protection from a court. The order of protection authorizes a summary arrest if the ex-husband initiates any contact with the woman. However, when the order of protection fails to prevent the ex-husband from assaulting or killing the woman, the police are sued on the theory that a special relationship had been created with the woman in that she relied on the police for protection.[8]

Vehicle pursuits have generated a substantial number of lawsuits against the police when the pursuit terminates in a collision that injures innocent bystanders, passengers in the pursued vehicle, or other motorists. Although the Supreme Court, in *County of Sacramento v. Lewis*, 523 U.S. 833 (1998), held that in federal civil-rights actions, police officers have qualified immunity for emergency decisions made during high-speed vehicle pursuits, plaintiffs can bring negligence or recklessness lawsuits in state courts for police failure to disengage from dangerous vehicle pursuits. Police liability for injuries result-

---

7. *Dwares v. City of New York*, 985 F.2d 94 (2d Cir. 1993).
8. *Raucci v. Town of Rotterdam*, 902 F.2d 1050 (2d Cir. 1990).

ing from efforts to apprehend escaping or resisting criminals places law enforcement in a dilemma. As the Circuit Court of Appeals has stated, "Lax law enforcement emboldens criminals and leads to more crime. Zealous pursuit of suspects jeopardizes bystanders and persons accompanying the offender. Easy solutions rarely work, and ex post assessments—based on sympathy for those the criminal has injured, while disregarding the risks to society at large from new restrictions on how the police work—are unlikely to promote aggregate social welfare."[9] *Mays v. City of East St. Louis*, 123 F.3d 999 (1997).

Among the newer theories being advocated before the courts are those that endeavor to hold the police responsible for their conduct prior to incidents in which they had to use deadly physical force. Although in such cases the plaintiffs concede that the officer had a right to defend himself from an armed criminal or a mentally disturbed person, they blame the officer for mishandling the approach to the situation. They advocate that police who violate their training or regulations should be liable for placing themselves in a position in which they were forced to defend themselves. To date, courts have not generally accepted this theory as a basis of liability. However, in a nation with a surplus of attorneys, new theories of liability will continually arise, and the police should expect to be the subject of many of them.

9. *Mays v. City of East St. Louis*, 123 F.3d 999 (1997).

CHAPTER EIGHT

Videotapes, Racism, and Police Brutality

With more and more people owning hand-held video cameras, an increasing number of incidents involving police use of force against citizens have been videotaped and aired on television news. The most infamous was the 1991 videotape of several Los Angeles police officers beating Rodney King after a high-speed car chase. The videotape showed the officers striking King numerous times with their nightsticks in an attempt to subdue and arrest him. The public's reaction to seeing an African-American man, lying on the ground, being beaten by several white police officers, was shock and abhorrence. Not since the images of Sheriff Bull Connor's German Shepherds snapping at civil rights demonstrators in Birmingham, Alabama, had the public been so outraged by apparent police brutality and racism. The public outcry after the King incident led to the indictment and trial of the officers in a California court. Their acquittal sparked the Los Angeles riots of 1991 and riots in other cities. After the California acquittal, the federal government indicted the officers for civil rights violations in connection with the incident, and two of the four officers were convicted and sentenced to prison.

On appeal, the convictions were reviewed and upheld by the United States Supreme Court in *Koon v. U.S.*, 518 U.S. 81 (1996). The Court summarized the facts:

> Rodney King and two of his friends sat in King's wife's car in Altadena, California, a city in Los Angeles County, and drank malt liquor for a number of hours. Then, with King driving, they left Altadena via a major freeway. King was intoxicated.
> California Highway Patrol officers observed King's car traveling at a speed they estimated to be in excess of 100 m.p.h. The officers followed King with red lights and sirens activated and ordered him by loudspeaker to pull over, but he continued to drive....

King left the freeway, and after a chase of about eight miles, stopped at the entrance to a recreation area. The officers ordered King and his two passengers to exit the car and to assume a felony prone position—that is, to lie on their stomachs with legs spread and arms behind their backs. King's two friends complied. King, too, got out of the car but did not lie down. Petitioner Stacey Koon arrived.... and as sergeant, Koon took charge. The officers again ordered King to assume the felony prone position. King got on his hands and knees but did not lie down. Officers.... tried to force King down, but King resisted and became combative, so the officers retreated. Koon then fired taser darts (designed to stun a combative suspect) into King.

The events that occurred next were captured on videotape by a bystander. As the videotape begins, it shows that King rose from the ground and charged toward Officer Powell. Powell took a step and used his baton to strike King on the side of the head. King fell to the ground. From the 18th to the 30th second on the videotape, King attempted to rise, but Powell and (Officer) Wind each struck him with their batons to prevent him from doing so. From the 35th to the 51st second, Powell administered repeated blows to King's lower extremities; one of the blows fractured King's leg. At the 55th second, Powell struck King on the chest, and King rolled over and lay prone. At that point the officers stepped back and observed King for about 10 seconds. Powell began to reach for his handcuffs....

At one-minute-five-seconds (1:05) on the videotape, (Officer) Briseno.... "stomped" on King's upper back or neck. King's body writhed in response. At 1:07, Powell and Wind again began to strike King with a series of baton blows, and Wind kicked him in the upper thoracic or cervical area six times until 1:26. At about 1:29, King put his hands behind his back and was handcuffed....

The judgment against the officers implied they should have stopped striking King, at the least, after the 55th second on the videotape, when King rolled over and lay prone. The blows struck after the 55th second were the primary factors for finding the officers guilty.

The King videotape has become a prominent historical record, and as a result almost any other videotape depicting alleged police brutality receives national media attention. The news media is in the business of airing controversial issues that will draw an audience, and they rarely, if ever, decline to show such videos. These videos rekindle the public's negative views of the police. Seeing a police officer striking, punching, or kicking a person produces a visceral reaction of repugnance. The public believes that no matter what the suspect's crime, the police should not hit him; the police should be able to do their job without beating people; they should find some other way to control the situation.

This reaction is essentially noble. It is ingrained in our culture. We do not want to see citizens being oppressed or abused by the agents of government. This ideal was expressed in our Declaration of Independence and the Bill of Rights, and has grown stronger over time. Since the civil rights movement and its exposure of historical and ongoing racism, the American public takes special offense when the person being abused is a member of a minority group.

Critics of the police have claimed that these videos exposed the American public to the ugly racism and brutality endemic in our police forces. In response, police defenders have tried to explain these incidents from the police point of view. They have attempted to point out the problems with assessing an incident based on videos that might not have captured the entire event or that were taken from a perspective or angle that distorted what actually occurred. But their defenses have been mainly ineffective. No amount of explaining or rationalizing can overcome the images of perceived police brutality. The issue is not about a rational analysis of the appropriate amount of force used in response to a particular risk. It is purely emotional and cultural. These video images have resurrected all the ugly scars of racism, and have exacerbated the pre-existing resentment of the police. Civil-rights groups and advocacy organizations, such as the National Association for the Advancement of Colored People and the American Civil Liberties Union, have offered them as evidence of a need to control the police and to require police departments to change their practices.

In response to a groundswell of allegations and complaints against the police after the King incident and efforts by civil rights organizations, Congress passed the Violent Crime Control and Law Enforcement Act of 1994, which authorized the Justice Department to file lawsuits against police departments that engaged in a pattern or practice of violating citizens' rights. As a result, court orders and consent decrees have imposed federal oversight of several police departments across the country, including the police departments of Los Angeles, Pittsburgh, Cincinnati, and Detroit.

Undoubtedly, thousands of alleged police brutality incidents occur across the nation, and those captured on videotape are only a minuscule fraction. Obvious questions need to be asked: Why do so many of these incidents occur? Are they always the fault of the police? Are a large number of police officers racist and/or brutal? Why has the substantial expenditure for police training failed to substantially reduce these kinds of incidents?

From the police side, the issues are clear. They have been sworn to uphold the law. They have been hired and empowered to make arrests based on the probable cause standard, and they can use reasonable force to effect an arrest when necessary. These incidents arise when people resist arrest or fail to comply with lawful directions. Officers who encounter persons who refuse to comply with directions or to be handcuffed do not know the motivation for the resistance. An officer cannot read a suspect's mind. The act of resisting arrest raises safety concerns, and an officer has an obligation to complete the arrest while protecting himself and the public. Moreover, police cannot allow people who resist arrest to succeed. Doing so would lead to disorder and chaos.

Police officers argue that in potentially violent situations, they need to take charge. They err on the side of caution because the stakes are so high. If they allow themselves to be overcome by a suspect, the suspect may take the officer's gun and use it to shoot the officer or someone else.

They argue that most people do not appreciate that when a suspect physically resists putting his hands behind his back, it is extremely difficult for an officer to successfully handcuff the suspect. When a suspect is stronger than the officer, when a suspect's adrenaline is pumping, it is almost impossible for an officer to force the wrists behind the back. Consequently, officers must resort to other means of physical force to convince suspects to comply. They may have to strike the suspect to disable him or to inflict enough pain to convince him to comply.

While there has been much discussion regarding police conduct, there has been sparse discussion or analysis regarding the public's side of the issue. Some obvious questions need to be answered. Why do so many citizens become involved in these incidents? Why do so many citizens resist arrest? Why do so many citizens refuse to comply with police directions? Why do so many citizens refuse to put their hands behind their backs and submit to handcuffing?

It is not because the citizens involved in these incidents are all mentally disturbed or violent criminals. Many, according to the lawsuits filed on their behalf, are law-abiding persons who happened to encounter abusive police officers. Others may have engaged in minor criminal activity, such as drug possession, petty theft, or simple assaults—not the kind of activity that should lead the police to have to use extreme force to subdue them.

Clearly, were citizens always willing to peacefully submit to arrest, the overwhelming majority of these incidents would not occur. Ideally, rational, law-abiding people do not resist arrest. They consent to the arrest, retain a lawyer, and address the charges in court. However, the fact remains that too many do resist. They may be intoxicated. They may be mentally unstable. They may be undergoing an episode of extreme emotional disturbance. They simply may be unable to accept the notion that they are going to be arrested. They may seek to avoid arrest because they are wanted on other charges or are in possession of unlawful drugs or a gun. They may be waiting for an opportunity to escape from the officer, or they may have intentions of assaulting the officer. The list of potential motivations is unlimited.

To deter individuals from resisting arrest, state legislatures enacted statutes that clearly mandate that people cannot use force to resist arrest, even if they feel the arrest is unjustified, and even if it later turns out that the arrest was unjustified. In New York, resisting arrest is a misdemeanor, punishable by a maximum of one year in prison.

The statute regarding the use of force to resist arrest is representative of the law in most states:

> A person may not use physical force to resist an arrest, whether authorized or unauthorized, which is being effected or attempted by a police officer or peace officer when it would reasonably appear that the latter is a police officer or peace officer.[1]

Resisting arrest and assault statutes are important and fundamental building blocks of our criminal justice system and our society. Despite their importance, they have not been enforced strictly enough to sufficiently instill in the public's mind the notion that resisting arrest and/or assaulting a police officer is an extremely serious violation of our norms and our value system. Some people perceive that a person can resist arrest, fight the police, curse at officers, or refuse to obey lawful directions, and, ultimately, not suffer a substantial penalty. They have justification to believe that the conduct will be excused. If arrested, the person may be acquitted. If an acquittal is unlikely, the court will often combine the resisting arrest charge with the primary charge that brought the person to police attention in the first place. This will occur either through plea-bargaining or through the imposition of concurrent sentences. As an example, in the case of a defendant who is convicted of charges such as grand larceny and resisting arrest, the judge may sentence the defendant to one year in prison for the grand larceny and one year for resisting ar-

---

1. *NY Penal Law*, Section 35.27.

rest. However, the sentences will run concurrently, so, in effect, the secondary resisting arrest charge will carry no penalty.

As a deterrent to resisting arrest or assaulting a police officer, legislatures should consider mandating that sentences for these offenses run consecutively to the underlying crime that instigated the arrest. A defendant's sentence for resisting arrest would not begin until the term of the sentence for the underlying crime was completed.

Over time, such legislation and its enforcement would instill a perception and belief that resisting arrest will not be tolerated. Assuming a cause and effect relationship between enforcement and deterrence, this should reduce instances of resisting arrest and the necessity for police to use force. Peaceful submission to arrest would become the norm, and, as a result, police would treat suspects with a greater degree of courtesy and care. Use of force to make an arrest would become the exception.

A reduction in the incidence of use of force would, of course, be beneficial in that fewer citizens and police officers would be injured. Furthermore, in situations calling for discretionary decisions by police whether to make an arrest or not, the absence of resistance will greatly increase the decisions not to arrest. Fewer incidents of force and fewer arrests would undoubtedly improve police relations with the communities that they serve and would reduce the antipolice bias that attorneys rely on to convince juries to punish or "pay back" the police for past transgressions.

CHAPTER NINE

The Exclusionary Rule and Tailored Testimony

Vociferous debate has raged for decades over the advantages and disadvantages of the exclusionary rule, which is the predominant legal technicality that affects the criminal justice process.

The exclusionary rule was not written in the Constitution or the Bill of Rights. It was first imposed in a federal court in 1914 in *U.S. v. Weeks.*, 232 U.S. 383, and then applied to the states in 1961 in *Mapp v. Ohio*. It is a judge-made rule that requires that evidence obtained in violation of constitutional standards be excluded from use against a defendant. Some of the violations include: unreasonable search and seizure; arrest without probable cause; interrogation of a suspect without giving Miranda warnings; questioning a suspect in the absence of his attorney; or conducting an improper lineup or other identification procedure.

Arguments and statistics have not resolved whether the exclusionary rule has provided any meaningful deterrence to police violations of constitutional rights. Putting aside that unresolved issue, the exclusionary rule, without doubt, causes three definite results. First, a certain number of guilty criminals escape justice. Second, police officers are encouraged to tailor their testimony to avoid the exclusion of evidence. Third, disrespect for the judicial system is fomented, which leads to police cynicism, lack of commitment, and, eventually, corruption. Each of these results adds to the problematic environment for police work that is so conducive to police-liability lawsuits.

By and large, the average police officer views the exclusionary rule as an unjust and unnecessary technicality that subverts the true purpose of law enforcement. In most cases in which it is applied, criminals unjustly go free or the charges against them are reduced. These results undermine belief in the integrity of the justice system. Although some officers may argue that the exclusionary rule is a necessary tool to maintain the integrity of the justice system, by far, most see it as an absurdity, or in common parlance, a joke. Judge

Benjamin Cardozo's famous facetious remark, "The criminal is to go free because the constable has blundered,"[1] still has resonance.

The difficulty created by the exclusionary rule cannot be attributed solely to the well-known Supreme Court cases that set forth broad definitions and concepts but also to cases from the lower federal, state, and local courts. Tens of thousands of cases are decided in the lower courts, and many of the decisions rendered are either erroneous or far exceed the mandates of the Supreme Court. The broad exercise of the exclusionary rule eradicates credible evidence from the truth-finding process. This may occur because a particular judge decides after-the-fact that a police action should have been conducted in a different manner. Chief Justice Earl Warren, although a leading figure in the defendant's rights movement, recognized the difficulties of second-guessing the police. He wrote, "A rigid and unthinking application of the exclusionary rule, in futile protest against practices which it can never be used effectively to control, may exact a high toll on human injury and frustration of efforts to prevent crime. No judicial opinion can comprehend the protean variety of the street encounter...."[2]

Many police officers would be surprised to learn that Justice Warren understood their predicament. They would be surprised, too, at the substantial dissenting opinion that exists regarding the Miranda rules for questioning suspects. Most officers believe and feel that *Miranda* and the thousands of cases emanating from it represent an incomprehensible and contradictory set of rules. Chief Justice Warren Burger articulated their feelings. In 1969, before he was appointed to the Supreme Court, Burger, in a dissenting opinion, predicted the difficulties *Miranda* would cause:

> The seeming anxiety of judges to protect every accused person from every consequence of his voluntary utterances is giving rise to myriad rules, sub-rules, variations and exceptions which even the most alert and sophisticated lawyers and judges are taxed to follow. Each time judges add nuances to these "rules" we make it less likely that any police officer will be able to follow the guidelines we lay down. We are approaching the predicament of the centipede on the flypaper—each time one leg is placed to give support for relief of a leg already "stuck," another becomes captive and soon all are securely immobilized. Like the hapless centipede on the flypaper, our efforts to extricate ourselves from this self-imposed dilemma will, if we keep it

---

1. *People v. Defore*, 242 NY 13 (1926).
2. *Terry v. Ohio*, 392 US 1 (1968).

up, soon have all of us immobilized. We are well on our way to forbidding any utterance of an accused to be used against him unless it is made in open court. Guilt or innocence becomes irrelevant in the criminal trial as we founder in a morass of artificial rules poorly conceived and often impossible of application.[3]

Justice Burger has been proved prescient. Since his warning, innumerable trial and appellate courts have allowed too many guilty criminals to go free.

In 1994, in *People v. Hampton*, 606 N.Y.S.2d 628, the New York Appellate Division reversed a guilty verdict based on the fact that a police officer had drawn his gun when he approached a suspect. The incident that led to the court ruling occurred after midnight on May 30, 1990, in the Bronx, New York. At that time, crime had been escalating and there had been a rash of gunpoint robberies of taxicab drivers. Many of the victims were shot and left for dead. In one year in New York City, fifty taxicab drivers were murdered. To address the problem, an association of Bronx taxicab drivers entered into an agreement with the police wherein the police would conduct safety checks of taxicabs carrying passengers, especially in areas prone to robberies.

Police Officers Kevin McGarvey and John Kennedy observed a cab with three male passengers in the back seat. McGarvey testified at a suppression hearing that the cab was being driven in an "erratic manner ... stopping in the middle of the block, starting to make turns, and then just kept going like he was lost." Suspecting a robbery, the officers followed the cab until it stopped at a corner. Hampton, the suspect, emerged from the rear passenger door, carrying a thin, white plastic bag that appeared "weighed" down by a heavy object. The officers left their vehicle and drew their guns. They told Hampton to stop. McGarvey approached and saw the outline of an Uzi-type machine gun through the plastic bag. He directed Hampton to put the bag down. When Hampton complied, the bag fell open, exposing the gun. The two other passengers fled, leaving two more guns on the floor of the cab.

The officers arrested Hampton. The Uzi machine gun and twenty-nine live rounds of ammunition were found in the bag, and narcotics were found in his jacket. At the station house, a further search of the defendant revealed $4,701 in cash, and vehicle registration and insurance cards in the name of a woman whom Hampton initially claimed was his girlfriend. After investigation, it was discovered that the woman was not his girlfriend, but the documents belonged to a woman who had recently been murdered during a robbery.

---

3. *Frazier v. United States*, 419 F.2d 1161, 1176 (1969).

Hampton waived his Miranda rights and gave incriminating admissions regarding the murder of the woman and regarding another woman also murdered during a robbery. Lineups were conducted and Hampton was identified in connection with the two murders.

During criminal proceedings in which Hampton was charged with two counts of murder in addition to the machine gun charge, his attorney made motion to suppress the evidence, claiming the stop of Hampton was an unreasonable search and seizure in violation of the Fourth Amendment. He claimed that the Uzi should be excluded from evidence, and, under the fruits of the poisonous tree doctrine, all subsequent evidence obtained as a result of the unlawful arrest should also be suppressed.

The trial judge denied the motions, and Hampton plea bargained and pled guilty to two counts of attempted murder, robbery first degree, and possession of unlawful narcotics. He was sentenced as a second-time felony offender to imprisonment from ten years minimum to twenty years maximum.

Not satisfied with the deal, Hampton appealed the trial judge's denial of his evidentiary suppression motions. He won. The Appellate Division of the New York Supreme Court, First Department, reversed the trial court rulings and held that the evidence should have been suppressed. The Court ruled that the "conduct of the police officers in this case constitutes an impermissible intrusion upon the privacy and security of the defendant ... requiring exclusion of the evidence seized."[4] Therefore, the guns, ammunition, narcotics, jewelry, documents and money, together with Hampton's incriminating statements and the lineup identification were all suppressed. Without direct testimony from the dead women, Hampton got away with the two murders.

The court reasoned that by drawing their weapons, the police escalated the situation from an investigation to a forcible stop. According to the New York State Criminal Procedure Law, a police officer may forcibly stop a person only "when he reasonably suspects that such person is committing, has committed or is about to commit ..." a crime.[5] The Court felt that the actions of the taxicab driver and the defendant were "susceptible of an innocent interpretation" and did not constitute reasonable suspicion. The Court did concede that "the circumstances in this case were sufficient to arouse interest and justify a request for information...."[6] Therefore the officers were justified in approaching the cab and the defendant, but were not justified in taking

---

4. *People v. Hampton,* 606 N.Y.S.2d 628, 629 (1994).
5. *NY Criminal Procedure Law,* section 140.50.
6. *People v. Hampton,* 606 N.Y.S.2d 628, 629 (1994).

out their guns. Had they kept their guns in their holsters until they actually observed the Uzi machine gun, the arrest and search would have been valid.

Of course, one could argue that had the officers kept their guns in their holders, Hampton or his accomplices might have shot and killed the officers.

Police officers exposed to these kinds of unjust court rulings may understandably develop a cynical view of the justice system, and cynical officers are not the best candidates for the difficult job of police work. They view the entire judicial process, from exclusionary rule hearings to liability judgments against them and their departments, as a fraud perpetrated against the public. To them, inconsistent and unrealistic rulings seem to be the norm. The frustrations of participating in a flawed system can discourage officers from energetically working to combat crime. For a few officers, the loopholes within the system represent opportunities for corruption. Under the exclusionary rules, an officer can easily tailor his testimony to convict or acquit, and some will do so for personal gain. For a substantial number of officers, the rules motivate them to tailor their testimony, whether consciously or unconsciously, in order to prevent guilty criminals from getting off because of legal technicalities. In their minds, changing a fact or two in order to avoid the suppression of evidence may seem necessary and justifiable. This is a dangerous game that can backfire.

Defendants in criminal cases will challenge police evidence in pretrial hearings to determine whether the evidence should be admitted or excluded. *Wade* hearings are held to determine whether the police conducted identification procedures in ways that were not overly suggestive; *Dunaway* hearings are held to determine whether police had probable cause to arrest a suspect; *Mapp* hearings determine whether there was probable cause to search; and *Huntley* hearings determine whether a statement to the police was made voluntarily.[7]

If, during one of these hearings, an officer's testimony is shown to be inconsistent or untruthful, the evidence will be excluded and the case most likely will be dismissed. The criminal defendant is then transformed into a potential civil court plaintiff with a perfect opportunity to sue for false arrest, malicious prosecution, unlawful detention, and violation of civil rights.

The following is a composite of a case in which concern for legal technicalities may have influenced testimony. Allegedly a robbery victim, near a

---

7. *U.S. v. Wade*, 388 U.S. 218 (1967); *Dunaway v. NY*, 442 U.S. 200 (1979); *Mapp v. Ohio*, 367 U.S. 643 (1961); *People v. Huntley*, 15 NY 2d 72 (1965).

parking lot in precinct A, was approached by a suspect who produced a gun and demanded the victim's wallet. The victim grabbed the gun. There was a struggle, and the gun went off and struck the suspect in the arm. The suspect fled and the victim called the police.

The suspect went to a hospital located in precinct B. Police from precinct B responded to the hospital where the suspect told them that he had been shot during an unrelated incident at a location different from the parking lot in precinct A.

Meanwhile, a detective from precinct A responded to the parking lot to interview the robbery victim. A short time later, he was notified that a person with a bullet wound (the suspect) was at the hospital in precinct B. He conveyed the victim to the hospital, where the victim saw the suspect on a stretcher and identified him as the person who had robbed him.

A lineup was not held, but the suspect was indicted on the basis of the hospital identification. Prior to the trial, the suspect's attorney made motions to exclude from evidence the hospital identification of the suspect by the victim and to exclude the statements the suspect made to the uniformed officer. A *Wade* hearing was held to determine whether the identification at the hospital was proper or overly suggestive and a violation of due process. In addition, a *Huntley* hearing was held to determine whether the statement that the suspect gave to the uniformed police was voluntary and in compliance with Miranda.

At the *Wade* hearing, the detective took the stand. He claimed his memory was not fresh and his notes did not help him remember the circumstances of the identification. Nevertheless, he testified to the best of his recollection that he had taken the victim to the hospital because the victim had complained of stress, might have had a heart condition, and had a gunpowder burn on his hand. He did not take him there to conduct an identification of the suspect, although he did say that he intended to interview the suspect at the hospital because he would be assigned to the case anyway. He claimed he considered the two cases as separate, unrelated incidents.

He testified that when he arrived at the hospital, there were no other police officers present. He sat the victim in a chair and went to get a nurse. He did not talk to the suspect. When he came back, the suspect was being pushed on a stretcher past the victim, and the victim made a spontaneous identification. The detective contended the identification was purely accidental.

The judge held his *Wade* ruling in abeyance, and proceeded with the *Huntley* hearing to determine whether the suspect's statements were voluntary.

At the *Huntley* hearing, the uniformed police officer from precinct B testified that he and his partner responded to the hospital, and while believing the suspect was the victim of a crime, took a voluntary statement from him. Then they radioed for a patrol car, a sergeant, and detectives from precinct A to respond. The patrol officers and the sergeant arrived first, so at least five uniformed officers were present when the detective arrived at the hospital. Contrary to the detective's testimony, the uniformed officer testified that the detective interviewed the suspect. He also testified that a few minutes later, with the uniformed police officers around the suspect, the stretcher was rolled past the victim, and he identified the suspect.

Two very different accounts: Which one is more believable?

Whether the detective's testimony was the result of poor memory, as he stated, does not change the effect of the two contradictory accounts. It is certainly understandable that a busy detective, handling several cases at once, might save steps and combine two investigations. Nonetheless, it surely could appear that his testimony was influenced by his partial knowledge of legal technicalities. He may have believed that to admit that uniformed officers surrounded the suspect would have resulted in the exclusion of the identification because it was done in a manner that was too suggestive and in violation of due process standards.

The officer should have attempted to refresh his recollection before testifying. If he could not recall the events, he should not have testified to anything of which he was not positive. By testifying to events of which he was unsure, he jeopardized not only the criminal case but also provided potential ammunition for a false-arrest lawsuit.

Ironically, the judge's *Wade* ruling made the identification issue moot. The judge ruled that since the suspect had not been arrested or placed in custody when he was on the stretcher and rolled past the victim, the identification occurred outside of police custody and the police were not yet responsible for providing due process protections. Consequently, the judge did not exclude the identification.

After the ruling, the suspect agreed to a plea bargain and pled guilty, a common occurrence in our criminal justice system. However, what may appear to be the end of the matter often is not. What routinely happens is that the suspect goes to prison while his lawyer appeals the ruling. If an appellate court overturns the trial judge's ruling, the conviction will be vacated and the case will be remanded for a new trial. Of course, at the new trial, the identification evidence will not be admissible, and the chances of conviction are greatly reduced. Time will have passed, and the district attorney may not be able to reassemble his witnesses. The case may result in a dismissal or an acquittal, which will allow the suspect to file suit for false arrest, and, perhaps, malicious prosecution, based on the contradictory testimony given by the detective and the uniformed officer.

Moreover, by the time the false arrest case approaches trial, the memories of the detective and the other officers will have faded even more. Years will have passed before the officers are subpoenaed, and the suspect's attorney will be able to further exploit the contradictions in their testimony. Of added significance will be the fact that the suspect, now deemed not guilty, will have spent time in prison for a crime he allegedly did not commit. If the lawsuit prevails, the jury may award a large amount of money, and the attorney will receive a third of the proceeds.

CHAPTER TEN

At the Trial

Though most police-liability lawsuits are settled before trial, a certain number do go to trial. These are usually serious cases with a potential for large damage awards, and they go to trial either because of genuine disagreements regarding the police conduct or because the settlement offer was not high enough. In these cases, a police-officer defendant faces an especially arduous task.

Officers are trained that it is their role as professional witnesses to testify objectively to firsthand observations and facts. They should not attempt to color factual testimony with their assumptions and certainly should not unfairly slant testimony. In a criminal trial, the credibility of a police officer's testimony is often the most important factor in the outcome.

In civil trials in which the police are the defendants, their credibility is even more critically important. In many of these trials, the facts are equally balanced, and credibility determines the jury's verdict. How officers conduct themselves can make or break a case. The standards for police are high, and jurors expect near perfection. One foolish statement, one off-color remark, could turn the case against the police. Inconsistent statements, or one lie, will destroy the police position.

Trial by jury is the ultimate test of a police officer's ability and professionalism. An officer may have made many street arrests and performed many other laudable duties, but our system requires that an officer justify his actions. To acquit himself well, an officer must not only study the factual content of the case, he must prepare himself as a worthy representative of his department and the law. During a trial, an officer must present a professional appearance—neat, clean, and composed. His demeanor should always be courteous and reflect a respect for the proceedings. He must realize that he is judged not only while he is on the witness stand but also from the moment he nears the courthouse. If he stops in a diner for breakfast before the court opens, a juror may be in the same diner and will notice him. In the halls of the courthouse, jurors may be nearby. If an officer is overheard talking about the case or making inappropriate or disparaging remarks, the jury will be aligned against him even before he testifies.

On the witness stand as a defendant in a civil action, an officer should employ, with some modifications, the same disciplines appropriate for testifying at criminal trials and at civil depositions. Listening carefully to the questions and answering appropriately without volunteering unnecessary information are essentials. He should not preface his answers with "to the best of my recollection" or "to the best of my knowledge." It is presumed he will answer to the best of his ability. If he does not know or does not recall, he should say, "I don't know" or "I don't recall." However, the overuse or misuse of these phrases as a method of avoiding questions will undermine his credibility in front of a jury. Knowing that his credibility can be more important than the factual issues of the case, he must endeavor to present himself as a person testifying in an honest, straightforward, and truthful manner.

At a civil trial, the plaintiff's attorney may call a police-officer defendant to the witness stand during the plaintiff's direct case. With the judge's approval, he may conduct the examination as a cross—using leading questions. This may be a tactical advantage for the attorney in that he controls the officer's initial testimony before the jury rather than waiting for the defense counsel to call the witness. Of course, during the defense case, the defense counsel may call the officer again. In such an event, the plaintiff's attorney will have another chance to cross-examine. For the officer this means he may be subjected to questioning twice by the plaintiff's attorney, and additionally if re-direct and re-cross are allowed.

Cross-examination is the method our justice system relies on to unearth truth. It has replaced trial-by-combat and trial-by-ordeal. Although less violent, it can be a devastating experience. Police-officer defendants have to understand what it takes to survive cross-examination. The examining attorney will likely employ tactics that have been developed over hundreds of years and proven to be effective at unearthing falsehood.

The cross-examining attorney will have a template for asking questions and building his case. Depending on what information has been developed during the discovery and deposition stages, he will vary his approach from witness to witness. When he believes the witness can establish facts that support his case, he will treat the witness respectfully, even when the witness is a defendant. Often, a witness' expected testimony will be favorable to the plaintiff in one part and adverse in another. In such cases, the attorney may employ the common technique of first exploring all areas of agreement in a relatively friendly manner before turning to areas of disagreement. In other cases, the attorney from the beginning may employ a contentious and aggressive line of questioning in an attempt to discredit or disparage the witness.

The testifying officer should try to maintain the same even-tempered demeanor throughout his testimony. He should not be argumentative with the plaintiff's attorney and agreeable with his own. While being questioned by the plaintiff's attorney, the officer should not answer so quickly that his attorney does not have an opportunity to object to the question. When an objection is raised, the officer should remain silent until advised whether or not to answer.

Although the examining attorney may speed up the pace of the questions, the police-officer witness should not be led into answering too quickly and before pondering the questions sufficiently. The officer can ask the attorney to slow down. When the attorney insists on yes or no answers, the officer should comply, unless a yes or no answer would be misleading. In such a case, the officer may ask the judge to allow him to explain.

A common tactic of cross-examining attorneys is to ask an officer about his background, e.g., how many years has he been a police officer, or a detective, or assigned to a special unit, or how many arrests has he made. The officer should answer these questions as briefly as possible and without any embellishment. The attorney asks these questions, not to build up the officer, but for the purpose of turning the answers against him. Whatever the officer's answer, the attorney will attempt to use it to discredit him. If the officer had made a large number of arrests, the attorney will try to portray him as overzealous. If the officer had made only a few arrests, the attorney will try to portray him as inexperienced or a laggard. The officer should anticipate this and maintain his equanimity in the face of the attorney's accusatory questions. Jurors tend to side with witnesses they see as being unfairly attacked. In this situation, turning the other cheek may be a winning strategy for the officer.

It is not unheard of that when a police officer takes the witness stand, the examining attorney questions him about statements he made in the hallway outside the courtroom to other officers or witnesses. This surprise tactic can be extremely disconcerting and often can fluster an officer, thereby diminishing him in the eyes of the jury. If an officer is aware of this possibility, he will be better able to respond in a controlled manner.

In lawsuits alleging an officer wrongfully fired his weapon, it is a common tactic for attorneys to question the officer about his failure to make an official statement during the preliminary investigation. Attorneys know full well that police superior officers and district attorneys generally will not question the officer because of constitutional and other legal considerations. Nevertheless, for the benefit of the jury, the attorneys will characterize the fact that the officer did not make an official statement as a refusal by the officer to answer questions, and they will imply that the officer did not voluntarily give a statement because he was engaged in a cover-up. The following is a composite example of how this line of questioning is routinely employed:

Q. Now, it's a fact, is it not, that whenever a shooting occurs, there is an official police department inquiry made of the officers who discharged their weapons; isn't that correct?

A. Yes.

Q. Now, in your particular case, they also conducted that inquiry, didn't they?

A. Yes.

Q. And you responded to that inquiry; didn't you?

A. As far as what?

Q. As far as that they questioned you under oath and you gave answers?

A. I don't understand what type of inquiry. There are different types of inquiry.

Q. Was there a time shortly after the shooting that you were placed under oath asked to answer questions?

A. No.

Q. No?

A. No.

Q. Isn't it a fact that higher police officials tried to question you within the first 48 hours and you refused to be questioned?

A. There is a 48-hour period.

Q. Yeah, there is a 48-hour rule.

A. There is a 48-hour period when officers that are involved in a shooting do not have to answer any questions.

Q. Right. You have that right in your contract; don't you?

Witness' Counsel: Objection.

Q. And you took advantage of that contract …

Witness' counsel: Objection.

Q. During the 48 hours where you refused to speak to higher police officials; you had an attorney and you consulted with counsel; did you not?

Witness' Counsel: Objection to the word refused, Judge.

Court: Yes or no? Did you have an attorney?

A. Not an attorney, no.

Q. You consulted with someone.

A. I had representation from my union at the scene and whoever made any inquiries did it through them.

Q. During the 48 hours where you refused to speak to higher police officials, did you nevertheless meet with the other officers who fired their weapons that day?

A. We met in the hospital.

Q. Did you talk to them about making sure that each of you had the same version events?

A. No, we did not.

Q. But during the 48 hours you met with every other officer who discharged his weapon?

A. We were all removed to the hospital.

Q. And it's your testimony that you didn't discuss among yourselves what your testimony would be?

A. Well, the sergeant was unconscious. The detective was on his back in the emergency room.

Q. Well, I just have one more question. Why did you insist on waiting for the 48 hours?

Witness' Counsel: Objection.

Q. Why didn't you talk to the police immediately?

Court: Sustained. Sustained. That is his prerogative, ladies and gentlemen, under the rules he did not have to answer questions.

Despite the judge's brief instruction to the jury that the officer did not have to answer questions, the impression was clearly planted by the plaintiff's attorney that the officer had refused to answer questions. On summation, the plaintiff's attorney would argue to the jury that the officer must have been hiding something otherwise he would have voluntarily told his superior officers about the circumstances of the shooting.

The officer's counsel could attempt to counteract the plaintiff's argument by explaining to the jury that most police departments have established rules for questioning officers after serious incidents, and, most important, he could explain that the district attorney decides whether an officer can be questioned and that the decision might not be made for weeks or months. Unfortunately, it is often difficult to erase the impression that the officer refused to answer questions.

The officer needs to emphatically state to the jury, "I did not refuse to answer questions." "No one asked me questions." "If my attorney had been present and advised me to answer questions, I would have."

Of course, the plaintiff's attorney might ask why the officer felt he needed an attorney. The answer is that police officers are not required to discard their constitutional rights, and any prudent citizen facing potential charges should consult with an attorney.

Ironically, the same attorneys, who defend criminals and who invoke their client's constitutional rights to counsel and to remain silent, attack police officers for exercising those same rights. They are able, by their powers of persuasion, to portray officers as having evaded questions when in fact the officers had not been questioned at all.

When a plaintiff attorney is able to combine the impression of an officer's evasiveness with inconsistencies in the officer's testimony, he will likely succeed in undermining an officer's credibility.

A plaintiff's attorney will surely confront an officer with the discrepancies in his statements. To protect himself, an officer should prepare by reviewing his deposition and his prior statements. When genuine inconsistencies exist, the officer should expect to be questioned about them and should have an adequate response. When the inconsistency is the result of an inadvertent error, he should simply admit it. When the inconsistency appears to indicate an intentional falsehood, the officer and his attorney must prepare a response that encompasses a true and plausible explanation, if possible.

If the examining attorney attempts to argue with the officer or to goad him into displaying anger, the officer must absolutely resist. He should not respond by attempting to argue or debate with the attorney. The officer will most likely lose, since the attorney makes his livelihood by argument and debate. Moreover, the officer should not allow himself to become angry. If he does, the attorney, during summation, will remind the jury of the officer's inability to control himself on the witness stand and will draw a line from the officer's conduct on the stand to the officer's conduct at the incident that precipitated the lawsuit.

Notwithstanding the need to remain in control of emotions, an officer may show emotions other than anger while on the witness stand. The officer could convey to the jury the true emotions he felt during the incident or after the incident. Communicating the fear, shock, surprise, confusion, or dismay he experienced can be more meaningful to a jury than the dry legalities of the case.

When given the opportunity, the officer should let the jury see that he is an ordinary person doing a difficult job. He should not attempt to impress anyone that police officers are in a special category. He should avoid police jargon and terminology but should explain his actions in plain language.

The jury system brings the human element and the common sense of ordinary citizens into the legal process. It is the role of the jury to interpret the facts, assess the credibility of witnesses, and to render a verdict in the name of society. It is incumbent on the officer, working with his counsel, to let the jury see his human face. He cannot allow his anger or frustration with the system or his disagreeable situation to prevent him from making contact with the members of the jury. The plaintiff's attorney will attempt to raise sympathy for the plaintiff and to portray the police and/or the police department as the callous, uncaring cause of the plaintiff's injuries. The officer, personally and as a representative of his department, must counteract the plaintiff's arguments by helping the jury understand the difficulties he faced during the incident that led to the lawsuit. He should convey to the jury that he takes his responsibilities seriously and that he acted to the best of his ability under the circumstances.

CHAPTER ELEVEN

What Police Agencies Should Not Do

Police agencies will respond to their increasing exposure to liability with administrative measures, more training, and further regulations. However, while doing so, they should be careful not to increase their exposure to liability by providing material for attorneys to use against them.

Overly Specific Written Regulations

Courts have held that law-enforcement agencies should have written rules and regulations as a means for supervision and direction of personnel, but courts generally defer to the administrative discretion of the agency regarding the details of the rules. Although written regulations are necessary to direct, instruct, and warn officers regarding policy and procedures, police agencies should employ great consideration before writing and adopting regulations that create stricter standards than legally necessary.

Internal department regulations, which do not reach the level of statutory authority, generally cannot establish clear legal duties that serve as a basis for civil-rights claims. Nonetheless, regulations are routinely relied on by expert witnesses to determine what proper and accepted police practices and procedures should have been applied in a particular case, and evidence of a violation of a pertinent regulation, although not controlling, can be considered as a factor in determining liability. Moreover, under state laws, failure to follow regulations can be a factor in determining negligent tort liability.

Police departments should promulgate strict and definite regulations to advise officers regarding acceptable standards of personal conduct, but instructions and advice regarding operational matters should be in the form of broad guidelines. General principles should be outlined; specific directions should not be given in detail. How much force to use in a given situation, or how to engage in a vehicle pursuit, or how to control a crowd cannot be dictated in advance.

Despite the understanding that guidelines should be broad, there has been an ever-increasing impulse to write more specific regulations. For example, in response to lawsuits as a result of injuries caused by police vehicle chases, many police departments have promulgated strict regulations regarding pursuit procedures. Clearly, vehicle pursuits should not be undertaken for minor offenses, and if the danger outweighs the risks of allowing the suspect to escape, a pursuit should be discontinued. However, police departments have gone beyond general principles and have written defined and detailed operational procedures. The procedures prohibit such tactics as paralleling, caravanning, boxing-in, or heading-off. It is certainly appropriate to educate officers to the dangers and the higher risk of injury that such tactics create, but it should be kept in mind that these tactics are not unlawful in themselves. The law is not so definite. Legislatures recognize that police face unanticipated dangers, and laws cannot be devised to provide exact instructions for every situation.

Legislatures have never passed a law mandating that police are liable because some of the police cars in a pursuit did not follow particular tactics. Yet, police departments have, in effect, usurped the legislature by promulgating definite regulations. As a result, when crashes and injuries occur during a police pursuit, attorneys are able to transfer the blame from the fleeing criminals to the pursing police officers.

Use of Force

Another example involves written regulations regarding the use of force. Most police departments and law-enforcement agencies across the country have promulgated extensive regulations regarding the use of firearms and other force, and many have revised their regulations several times. The New York City Police Department (NYPD), the largest police department in the nation, has repeatedly revised its regulations regarding use of force. Over several decades, these regulations have evolved from general principles to specific instructions, and some types of force have been absolutely prohibited.

Until 1972, the NYPD Rules and Procedures did not include prospective rules, regulations, or procedures regarding the use of physical force. They mandated only the equipment an officer must carry, e.g., a .38-caliber revolver, a baton, and handcuffs.

With respect to firing a weapon, Section 38.9 simply stated:

A member of the force who discharges a revolver except at an authorized range shall promptly notify the desk officer of the precinct of occurrence. The desk officer shall direct a superior officer to make an immediate investigation of the cause and effect of such discharge.

The New York State Penal Law was the basis for determining whether an officer was justified or unjustified in discharging his firearm.

In 1972, the NYPD Rules and Procedures were replaced by the Patrol Guide in which six specific directives were included. Although they were termed "guidelines," in fact, they were regulations. An officer who violated them could be disciplined or fired.

Use of Firearms, section 104-1 stated:

In addition to Penal Law restrictions on the use of deadly physical force (See Article 35.00 P.L.), members of the service will adhere to the following guidelines concerning the use of firearms:
1. Use all reasonable means before utilizing firearm when effecting arrest for or preventing or terminating a felony or defending self or another.
2. Do not fire warning shots.
3. Do not discharge firearm to summon assistance, except when safety is endangered.
4. Do not discharge firearm from or at moving vehicle unless occupants are using deadly physical force against officer or another, by means other than vehicle.
5. Do not discharge firearm at dogs or other animals unless there is no other way to bring animal under control.
6. Do not discharge firearm if innocent persons may be endangered.

The intention of these guidelines was to reduce shooting incidents by police. Instead, the guidelines had the unintended consequence of providing lawyers with a new field of litigation in which they could second-guess officers.

Guideline 1 discarded the penal law standard of reasonable belief and imposed a stricter standard in that the arrest, prevention, or termination must have been in connection with conduct that was a felony. This guideline implies that after a shooting if the purported felony turned out to be a misdemeanor or not a crime, then the officer violated the Patrol Guide.

The guideline also provided the grounds for lawyers to argue that a police officer was derelict because he did not use "all reasonable means" before using his gun. In hindsight, it is always easy to say someone should have done something differently.

Guideline 6 was especially faulty. It abrogated an officer's inherent common law and statutory right of self-defense. According to guideline 6, an officer under attack by a group of persons using deadly physical force against him cannot use his weapon to defend himself if other persons are near or behind the attackers. The law does not require such a sacrifice.

In 1991, the Patrol Guide was amended further in response to such cases as *Tennessee v. Garner* and *McCummings v. NYC Transit Authority*, and new restraints were added, such as:

Section, 104-1:

b.   The firearm shall be viewed as a defensive weapon, **not** a tool of apprehension.

c.   Every other reasonable alternative means will be utilized before a police officer resorts to the use of his firearm.

Within three years, the New York City Police Department was inundated with lawsuits, and it was realized that the 1972 and 1991 guidelines were ill conceived and needed modification.

In 1994, Patrol Guide section 104-1 was amended again. Guideline 1 was changed to mirror the penal law standard of "probable cause" and to eliminate the requirement to "use all reasonable means before utilizing firearm."

The new guideline stated:

(b) Police officers shall not use deadly physical force against another person unless they have probable cause to believe they must protect themselves or another person present from imminent death or serious physical injury.

This guideline re-authorized police officers to act in accordance with the powers invested in them by New York State law.

Guideline 6 was modified by adding the word, "unnecessarily."

The new guideline stated:

(c) Police officers shall not discharge their weapons when doing so will unnecessarily endanger innocent persons.

This guideline re-invested police officers with the same right of self-defense that all people possess. When necessary to defend themselves against deadly force, they may do so even if innocent persons might be endangered.

In addition, the 1994 revisions eliminated the 1991 amendments that had prohibited the firearm as a tool of apprehension and that had mandated the use of all other reasonable alternative means before resorting to the use of the firearm even in self-defense.

The 1994 guidelines were an improvement over the previous guidelines. Lawyers could no longer use the flawed prohibitions and mandates to argue that their violation amounted to negligence. To show wrongful conduct by a police officer in self-defense situations, they now had to prove the officer acted without probable cause or unnecessarily fired his weapon. These are factual issues that must be argued on the basis of real world experience, not semantic violations of poorly worded regulations.

Notwithstanding the above improvements, the 1994 amendments continued the severe restrictions regarding the use of force when attempting to prevent felonies or arrest fleeing felons. Patrol Guide, section 104-1 (d), which was renumbered in 2000 to section 203-12 (d), mandated:

> (d) Police officers shall not discharge their firearms to subdue a fleeing felon who presents no threat of imminent death or serious physical injury to themselves or another person present.

This mandate goes far beyond the requirements of *Tennessee v. Garner*, which specifically allowed police officers to shoot a fleeing criminal who committed a crime involving the infliction or threatened infliction of serious physical harm. The section contravenes the penal law authority granted to police. The New York State Penal Law authorizes a police officer to use deadly force to arrest for a felony:

> ... involving the use or attempted use or threatened imminent use of physical force against a person; or ... kidnapping, arson, escape in the first degree, burglary in the first degree or any attempt to commit such a crime.[1]

Currently, an NYPD officer who shoots an unarmed fleeing robber, kidnapper, child molester, rapist, or arsonist will violate his own department's procedures, and will, thereby, place himself in jeopardy of civil liability.

The consequences of this prohibition upon police officers is further illustrated by the fact that ordinary citizens now have more license to use deadly force than police officers.

New York State Penal Law states:

> A private person acting on his own account may ... use deadly physical force ... when he reasonably believes such to be necessary to ...

---

1. *NY Penal Law*, Section 35.30-1.

effect the arrest of a person who has committed murder, manslaughter in the first degree, robbery, forcible rape or forcible criminal sex-
ual act and who is in immediate flight therefrom.[2]

Under these conditions, if a law-abiding family is in their home at night,
and a criminal burglarizes the home, forcibly rapes a woman in the home,
and attempts to flee, a family member can pursue the criminal and shoot
him to prevent his escape. A responding New York City police officer is prohibited by his department rules from doing the same thing.

An officer who shoots a fleeing burglar-rapist is not likely to be prosecuted
for assault because the penal law authorizes such use of force, but he could
be liable for civil damages.

The word among the police is that unless someone is attacking them,
they will not use their guns to make an arrest, no matter how horrendous
the crime from which the criminal is escaping. Criminals know this. They
know it is foolish to submit to arrest and to be caught in the immediacy of
their crime with telltale evidence on their person. If they can outrun or
out-drive the police, they will. It is highly unlikely that police officers will
risk their careers and personal assets by shooting. This may be the result
that the city administrators want, but it may not be the result that the citi-
zenry expects.

Choke Holds

Another NYPD Patrol Guide regulation that provides additional material
for attorneys to use in lawsuits is the prohibition of choke holds.

Patrol Guide, Use of Force, Procedure 203-11, mandates:

> Members of the New York City Police Department will **NOT** use
> chokeholds. A chokehold shall include, but is not limited to, any pres-
> sure to the throat or windpipe, which may prevent or hinder breath-
> ing or reduce intake of air.

The absolute prohibition of choke holds goes far beyond any legislative restraint on the use of force. This administrative prohibition, in effect, has created a strict liability cause of action. In a civil lawsuit, if an officer caused injury by using a choke hold, his violation of the departmental regulation
would provide almost indefensible proof of liability.

---

2. *NY Penal Law*, Section 35.30-4.

In the areas of use of force, self-defense, and emergency action, police departments should not write such absolute prohibitions. Instructions cannot be devised for all police situations. Without question, police officers should not employ a choke hold when it is unnecessary, when less dangerous means will suffice to gain control of a subject, or when an officer or a third party is not in serious danger. But, across the nation, thousands of incidents have occurred in which police officers have fought with criminals or emotionally disturbed persons who were extremely strong and dangerous. In too many of these situations, the criminals have killed or seriously injured the police officers. On a recurring basis, criminals have overpowered officers, taken their guns, and shot them with their own police weapons. In a life and death physical struggle, a choke hold might be the only effective means an officer has to defend himself. To absolutely prohibit an officer from using a choke hold under such circumstances contravenes the inherent right of self-defense. Furthermore, the prohibition may dissuade an officer in the midst of a struggle with an assailant from acting quickly enough to preserve his own life by employing a choke hold. Regulations regarding use of force should always include a contingency for situations when an officer's life is in danger.

The issue cannot be dismissed by the notion that a jury would not find liability against an officer whose life was nearly lost in a struggle, since the issue will arise only when an officer has succeeded in using a choke hold to defend himself. In court, a surviving officer will find it extremely difficult to prove the necessity for its use. The plaintiff's attorney will point to the absolute prohibition against choke holds, and the jury may find the officer liable.

Emotionally Disturbed Persons

Another area of police responsibility that has evolved into a fertile area for lawsuits is the handling of emotionally disturbed persons. The older New York City Police Department Rules and Procedures did not mandate specific tactics. Section 10, relying on the authority of the Mental Hygiene Law, simply stated:

> A mentally ill person not already in safekeeping shall be taken into custody and brought to the station house.
> And
> An officer shall use restraining equipment on a psychiatric patient:
> (a). If the patient is violent, disorderly, or resists ...

Over a period of years, the NYPD Patrol Guide procedure regarding Mentally Ill or Emotionally Disturbed Persons (EDP) was extensively revised. In the 2000 revision, six pages of directions were issued, including definitions, potential circumstances, and the exact actions to be taken in each circumstance.

Section 216-05-1 states:

> 1. Upon arrival at scene, assess situation as to threat of immediate serious physical injury to EDP, other persons present, or members of the service. Take cover, utilize protective shield if available and request additional personnel, if necessary.
> a. If emotionally disturbed person's actions constitute immediate threat of serious physical injury or death to himself or others:
> (1). Take reasonable measures to terminate or prevent such behavior. Deadly physical force will be used only as a last resort to protect the life of persons or officers present.
> b. If EDP is unarmed, not violent and is willing to leave voluntarily:
> (1). EDP may be taken into custody without the specific direction of a supervisor.
> c. In all other cases, if EDP's actions do not constitute an immediate threat of serious physical injury or death to himself or others:
> (1). Attempt to isolate and contain the EDP while maintaining a **zone of safety** until arrival of patrol supervisor and Emergency Service Unit personnel.
> (2). **Do not attempt to take EDP into custody without the specific direction of a supervisor.**

This poorly constructed section requires an officer to make several judgments. In practice, these judgments can often be mistaken and subject to criticism. While the concepts and purposes underlying these regulations are good, the regulations should be generalized and not written as absolute rules. Since the section is written in such an unqualified fashion and contains categories that do not cover every practical situation, it provides lawyers with potent material to attack an officer's actions.

Difficulty arises for officers when they make a judgment, begin to take action based on that judgment, and the circumstances suddenly change. For instance, regarding section b. (1): if an officer observes an unarmed, non-violent EDP who appears willing to be taken to the hospital, the officer may approach the EDP without a supervisor's permission. On the officer's approach, however, the EDP may suddenly turn violent, or run toward a window, or grab a dangerous object. In reaction, the officer may have to use force to restrain the EDP. If the EDP is injured, then the officer faces potential liability.

Questions will be asked about the officer's assessment. Did the officer interview people who knew the EDP to ascertain whether he could be violent? Was the officer properly trained in recognizing the different types of EDP? Why did he not take cover behind a protective shield? Why did he not call for additional personnel? Why did he not call for the supervisor? Why did he not maintain a zone of safety? Why did he attempt to take the EDP into custody without permission of the supervisor? Why did he not use alternative means of force?

Lawyers can have a field day with this kind of material. In many cases involving the use of force against an emotionally disturbed person, police officers are placed in an untenable position. They must explain the reasons for their actions, but their reasons may not coincide with the written regulations. What was a common sense decision or a natural response during the encounter becomes a violation.

To summarize, police agencies, in an effort to limit their own liability, should not write detailed regulations that create whole new fields of litigation. Police regulations regarding use of force and arrest powers should mirror the laws that authorize those powers. Officers should be thoroughly trained in proper police practices and procedures, and any officers who persist in violating those practices and procedures should be disciplined or dismissed, as appropriate. However, it is not beneficial to promulgate artificial and unrealistic regulations that provide further opportunities for lawyers to extract money from police departments and police officers.

Chapter Twelve

What Police Agencies Should Do: Seven Recommendations

The following recommendations admittedly are similar to many that have been proposed before, especially those pertaining to administrative matters and the need for documentation. However, these recommendations differ where they attempt to address the need to recognize that the police are under attack by aggressive, ambitious attorneys who are bent on undermining the police mission, and they differ where they attempt to address the issues of police attitudes and values that are so important for a healthy and successful law-enforcement community.

1. Training

Law enforcement has the responsibility to protect its lawful operational authority and to protect its officers from unjustified lawsuits without surrendering its ability to combat violent crime. It must recognize how and why police-liability lawsuits arise, do more to train police officers to prevent and avoid them, and when necessary, defend against them.

Training should be ongoing and should involve more than the dissemination of information through lectures or handouts. The best interactive educational methods should be employed, such as role-playing and video simulations. Periodic testing should be conducted to ensure that officers have absorbed the information and can articulate what training and information they have received. Many lawsuits against the police allege negligent training by the agency, and attorneys will attempt to prove their claims by questioning officers. When the officers cannot recount the type, amount, or content of the training they have received, they help the attorneys build a case against the agencies. Police agencies, by testing officers and maintaining records of their test results, can demonstrate that they have instituted and maintained high standards of training.

In a case in which a police department was sued for the death of an emotionally disturbed man in their custody, the department attempted to defend itself by offering records of all the extensive training sessions and comprehensive material they had provided to their officers regarding the proper handling of emotionally disturbed persons. However, when the supervisor on duty when the death occurred was asked whether he received such training, he testified, "No. I honestly don't recall any, no."

2. Provide Sufficient Resources for Arrest Processing

Police departments should allocate the necessary time and resources for arresting officers to properly prepare their cases. Most departments operate under limited budgets and attempt to control the amount of overtime their officers incur, but overtime constraints should not overrule the requirements of court presentation. One large monetary judgment against the department as a result of an inadequately prepared case will wipe out years of overtime savings.

In most jurisdictions, defendants who are ineligible for release with a desk appearance ticket or a summons must be arraigned within twenty-four hours of arrest. This requirement pressures arresting officers to rush through their paperwork in order to deliver the defendant to court within the deadline. To avoid mistakes in the paperwork, police managers should establish alternative procedures or assign additional officers to assist the arresting officer when necessary.

3. Ensure Proper Prosecutions of Arrests

Police agencies need to establish policies, customs, and practices that will counteract the arrest-and-forget-it mentality. In large police departments, more so than smaller departments, officers may act as though their job is finished when the arrest is made and they have turned over the defendant to the court system. Police departments should instill in their officers a sense of responsibility for the entirety of the case. Ideally, all officers will accept their responsibilities; in reality, a percentage will not. Some officers cynically view the "broken" justice system as beyond their concern. They will not adequately maintain interest in old cases, and will not sufficiently prepare for depositions or civil trials.

Police managers must recognize these shortcomings and implement measures to facilitate proper documentation, record keeping, and case preparation. Systems should work for both dedicated officers and for officers who may have less than a full commitment to their responsibilities.

Procedures should be implemented to ensure that all appropriate criminal charges are filed against defendants, all evidence and witnesses are presented, and cases are not inadvertently or unjustifiably dismissed. When an officer without firsthand knowledge is assigned to process an arrest, it should automatically follow that the officer or the witness with direct knowledge provides a supporting affidavit to the district attorney. Police agencies should have their officers available for meetings with district attorneys and municipal law departments, and should adhere strictly to court schedules. A case should never be lost because an officer is on vacation.

4. Ensure Documentation of Probable Cause

Supervisors need to verify that reports prepared by their officers include full and complete accounts of the incident and the factual observations necessary to establish the probable cause for the arrest. They need to ensure that statements of defendants and witnesses are recorded or noted. Well-documented, preserved, and available evidence is the key to heading off false arrest lawsuits. The importance of this cannot be overstated because a sustained false arrest claim is usually the necessary predicate to support the most serious claims of excessive use of force. A small piece of preserved evidence, such as a note of a witness' statement that established probable cause, can prevent or defeat a lawsuit.

Probable cause can be based on hearsay evidence. Such evidence, unless an exception applies, may be inadmissible in a criminal trial to prove a defendant's guilt, but hearsay can be important and admissible in a civil trial to prove the police acted with probable cause. Therefore, officers must identify witnesses who made statements to them, even brief informal statements made on the street. During the course of certain incidents to which police have been called, it is clear to everyone present that a particular person should be arrested. Witnesses make comments to the police officers. The police make an arrest, and the witnesses assent to the police action. However, later on, it is difficult to find those witnesses in order to have them testify. As a result, the criminal case is sometimes dismissed and a lawsuit for false arrest is filed. So officers must make notes of all witness statements contemporaneously or as soon as possible after they are made. In court, such contemporaneous notes may be used to refresh an officer's recollection and, in some circumstances, the notes themselves may be introduced as evidence.

In search warrant situations, standard practice is to assign one officer to record the evidence or contraband found and where it was found. An additional officer should be assigned to record statements made by persons present during the execution of the search warrant and to note whether the statements were spontaneous or in response to direct questioning.

5. Reestablish Semi-Military Discipline and Supervision

Police-liability lawsuits can be brought against individual supervisors for acts or omissions related to tort and civil-rights violations committed by officers under their command. Lawsuits can also be brought against the municipality for patterns and practices of inadequate discipline and supervision that contributed to or caused the violations. Obviously, most police departments endeavor to maintain satisfactory discipline and to employ good supervisory practices as the best means of preventing such lawsuits. Most police departments have implemented procedures for mandatory investigation of all complaints of improper police conduct and have implemented early-warning programs to identify officers who may be undergoing psychological stress and who may become problem employees. Nonetheless, police departments and municipalities have lost many lawsuits on the basis of negligent discipline or negligent supervision claims and have been forced to settle many others. In response, they have increased written regulations and imposed stricter administrative penalties for violations of the regulations. These defensive measures have failed to reduce the number of lawsuits. Although they are designed to protect the agency, they are negative in nature and do not establish the kind of positive, internalized discipline required for the police profession.

Police departments need to return to the traditional semi-military style of police management that was common after the Second World War when police superiors with military experience dominated the field and maintained a high degree of positive discipline. Regrettably, the opposite has been the trend. Large and small police departments have participated in the societal changes that have swept across society, including a loss of respect for authority, a lessening of accountability for language and behavior, and a weakening of traditional moral values. Police departments, concurrent with these societal changes, have lowered the standards of personal comportment, relaxed the day-to-day supervisory climate, and moved away from the military style. Basic military protocols, such as saluting or wearing the uniform hat, have been abandoned along with the military traditions of loyalty and duty.

Unlike the military where commissioned officers are trained at West Point, Annapolis, or other officer-training schools, police superiors come from the ranks. In the past, this was an advantage for police departments because police supervisors had years of experience, rather than coming directly out of school. However, in the 1970s many police departments reduced the years in rank required for promotion to sergeant, lieutenant, and captain, and the traditional age and experience differences between superior officers and the ranks below them has been all but eliminated. In many departments, a high degree of fraternization exists between supervisors and officers, and sergeants often act, not as supervisors but simply as another officer. Various programs such as team policing or community policing have flattened organizational structures and have blurred the lines of communication and the chain of command. Consequently, hands-on, direct, and appropriate discipline has been softened.

A lack of distinction between supervisors and officers, along with other factors, can be used by plaintiff attorneys to prove claims of negligent discipline or supervision. Establishing that sergeants regularly socialize with officers, carpool with them, go drinking with them, or acquiesce to minor rules violations, will help prove the claim. In *Gutierrez-Rodriguez v. Cartagena*, 882 F.2d 553 (1989), a police supervisor was found liable for the conduct of his subordinate who shot a civilian. The supervisor knew that the subordinate had been the subject of a number of citizen complaints and had a reputation for having a violent character in mistreating citizens. The supervisor and the subordinate were friends and testimony indicated that the supervisor was less strict with him than with other officers. On one or two occasions the supervisor assigned the subordinate to a desk job, but the subordinate demanded to be returned to the street, and the supervisor complied.

The supervisor was found jointly liable with his agency for a judgment of $4.5 million in favor of the plaintiff. In addition, he was found personally liable for punitive damages of $225,000.

A well-established culture of a strong, semi-military organization will tend to prevent circumstances of compromised supervision, and evidence of professional management practices can disprove claims of negligent supervision. More important, traditional modes of strict supervision may, indeed, prevent the kinds of conduct and mistakes that lead to catastrophic lawsuits.

6. Provide Legal Education

Law-enforcement officials must address the problems associated with the exclusionary rule and other legal technicalities. Although it would be unrealistic to believe that officers could be convinced of the appropriateness of the exclusionary rule and the other myriad technicalities in the judicial process, they must be educated about the historical development of our judicial system. They must be inculcated with the importance of the role they play in the system, and they must understand that failure to execute their responsibilities with absolute integrity, commitment, and competency provides ammunition for their adversaries. They cannot merely do an adequate job; they must perform to the highest standards.

Police officers must not attempt to adjust their testimony in order to make the present system work. Any hint of police perjury or other misconduct adds fuel to the movement to further restrict police authority and discretion. Paradoxically, when officers testify truthfully to actions they have taken in good faith and their testimony results in the exclusion of evidence and the dismissal of cases against guilty defendants, in the long run it is beneficial. When enough criminal cases are dismissed and the public comes to realize that the police cannot adequately perform their functions without coming into conflict with the exclusionary rule, judicial reform will follow. In fact, a fair amount of reform has already occurred. The Supreme Court has issued several important rulings that have modified prior cases that called for the absolute and strict implementation of the exclusionary rule. In *U.S. v. Leon*, 468 U.S. 897 (1984), the Court established the good faith exception to the warrant requirement. The Court held that evidence obtained on the basis of a search warrant that was later determined to be invalid may be admitted into evidence at trial if the police officer who conducted the search relied on the warrant in "good faith."

In *U.S. v. Havens*, 446 U.S. 620 (1980), the Supreme Court ruled that a defendant's confession taken without proper Miranda warnings, though not admissible as evidence-in-chief to prove the government's case, may, nevertheless, be used to impeach the testimony of a defendant.

In *New York v. Quarles*, 467 U.S. 649 (1984), the Court established the public safety exception to the Miranda warning requirement. In *Quarles*, police officers who arrested a man for rape asked him where he had discarded a gun. The arrest took place in a supermarket, and the assailant was thought to have concealed the gun somewhere inside the store. The Court said, "The need for answers to questions in a situation posing a threat to the public safety outweighs the need for the prophylactic rule protecting the Fifth Amendment's privilege against self-incrimination."

In 1984, the Court established the inevitable discovery exception to the fruits of the poisonous tree doctrine. The impetus for this exception was the famous case of the Christian burial speech. On Christmas Eve, 1968, Robert Williams, in a YMCA in Des Moines, Iowa, murdered a ten-year-old girl, Pamela Powers. He took the body and left the area. Two days later, aided by an attorney, Williams surrendered to the police in Davenport, Iowa, 160 miles from Des Moines. The attorney advised the detectives not to question Williams on the automobile trip back to Des Moines. However, knowing Williams was a former mental patient and deeply religious, one of the detectives, without directly questioning him, made a speech with religious overtones to induce Williams to show them where the little girl's body was buried. Williams responded and led them to the body.

At his first trial, Williams was convicted, but the Supreme Court ruled in *Brewer v. Williams*, 430 U.S. 387 (1977) that the burial speech was an unlawful interrogation in violation of the right to counsel, so the evidence of the body had to be excluded from evidence, and Williams was given a second trial.

The second trial was held, and the defendant was convicted again. The second conviction was also appealed, but this time the conviction was upheld. The Supreme Court, in *Nix v. Williams*, 467 U.S. 431 (1984), overturned its prior decision in *Brewer v. Williams* and held that the evidence of the body was admissible because the search party would have inevitably discovered the body, even without the assistance of the defendant.

These cases demonstrate that the courts will eventually adjust the rules to accord with the realities and practical problems that police encounter. If the police continue to present honest testimony of their actions taken in good faith, more aspects of the exclusionary rule will be modified, though the process may take decades.

In the meantime, officers can be trained to handle the practicalities of today's exclusionary rule. They must learn, as well as possible, the rules of search and seizure, interrogation, and identification. In addition, they must learn that the exclusionary rule does not apply in civil cases, and that evidence, excluded during a criminal case, may be admissible in a civil case. For example, voluntary statements by defendants who did not receive Miranda warnings may be admissible at a civil trial and can be extremely powerful evidence.

It is important that officers understand the broader uses of evidence in civil trials and how imperative it is to preserve all evidence, even that excluded from a criminal prosecution. This knowledge should reinforce the importance of getting witness statements, taking notes, making accurate reports, and collecting and preserving physical evidence. These are the battlefield tactics that police can use against criminal-defense attorneys and perhaps at a later date to defeat police-liability lawyers.

7. Instill Professionalism

The overwhelming majority of police officers perform their duties in an excellent manner—most of the time. Unfortunately, even a small error rate can create substantial problems for the officers and their departments. It takes only a small number of badly performing officers to discredit the accomplishments of the majority and to incite the antipolice rhetoric that is so detrimental to the police mission. Therefore, it is imperative that law-enforcement agencies commit the time and resources to personnel management. This commitment cannot be perfunctory; it must be genuine and extraordinary.

Police administrators must take on the role of educators, mentors, even moral philosophers in order to help young officers deal with the difficulties and stresses of police work. With the assistance of professionals from outside law enforcement, they need to establish open communications with the officers under their charge and to address the cynicism that undermines each new generation of officers. Most officers, like most young people, begin their careers with positive goals and high ideals, but a few years of police work can destroy it all.

A percentage of officers feel that they have been alienated from the public by judicial and political systems that fail to support them. The loss of faith in higher authority leads to an us-against-them mentality, and corruption of all kinds, at all levels.

Police administrators must endeavor to keep officers committed to the search for justice, which is one of the most powerful motivating factors of human endeavor. It is why many choose to become law-enforcement officers. Justice includes the concepts of fairness, right, equality, impartiality, duty, and responsibility. Officers need to understand and appreciate these concepts, so they can offset the cynicism they encounter and can motivate themselves to maintain the highest levels of integrity. They need to gain perspective and view the world from a higher plain.

That being said, police officers still need to deal with the realities of our current judicial process. Arresting people, searching and handcuffing them, and using physical force are high stakes activities that can have substantial consequences. Physical injuries can occur to either officers or suspects. Under certain circumstances, criminal sanctions can be imposed on an officer, who is unlikely to avoid a conviction because of a technicality. If charged, he will need to prove his innocence. On the other hand, suspects may avoid convictions and penalties when it is deemed that the police violated their constitutional rights.

Men and women who choose a police career, knowing the rules and knowing the risks, would be remiss to approach the job with less than a full commitment to excellence. It would be unfair to themselves, to their families, and to their departments. Recognizing the adversarial nature of the judicial process, they must acquire the knowledge and skills necessary to play their parts in a professional and positive manner.

Armed with the knowledge of the tactics and strategies that adversarial attorneys use to subvert the efforts of law enforcement, police officers will more ably resist and counteract them. Officers should consider it an essential duty to prepare themselves for the rigors of deposition and cross-examination, since preparation will result in fewer successful lawsuits against them and their departments. Fewer successful lawsuits, no doubt, will reduce the number of lawsuits filed, and will allow police officers to focus on their primary duties with less fear of becoming embroiled in litigation and less fear of career and financial ruin.

Index